MY JOURNEY WITH HOLY SPIRIT

THROUGH CANCER & OTHER BATTLES

JILL FALCO

WRITTEN BY
JONATHAN MACNAB

My Journey with Holy Spirit

Copyright © 2023 by Jill Falco and Jonathan Macnab

All rights reserved. No part of this book may be reproduced in any form or by any electronic or mechanical means, including information storage and retrieval systems, without permission in writing from the publisher, except by reviewers who may quote brief passages in a review.

Unless otherwise noted, all Scripture references are taken from the New King James Version®. Copyright © 1982 by Thomas Nelson. Used by permission. All rights reserved.

ISBN 978-1-7320417-6-9

First Printing, 2023

Story Reborn Publishing
170 Pikesville Rd.
Fulton, MS 38843

www.storyreborn.com

This title is also available as an e-book at most online retailers.

> "Ears to hear and eyes to see—both are gifts from the Lord."
> — Proverbs 20:12, NLT

> "Then David said to the Philistine, 'You come to me with a sword, with a spear, and with a javelin. But I come to you in the name of the Lord of hosts, the God of the armies of Israel, whom you have defied. This day the Lord will deliver you into my hand, and I will strike you and take your head from you... for the battle is the Lord's'"
> — 1 Samuel 17:45-47

Table of Contents

Foreword	1
Preface	2
Chapter 1 – He Is With You	4
Chapter 2 – Who Fights My Battles?	14
Chapter 3 – A Hidden Conflict	32
Chapter 4 – Don't Go to Sleep	41
Chapter 5 – Awakening	56
Chapter 6 – Becoming a Child	74
Chapter 7 – Fight Song	91
Chapter 8 – Never Back Down	100
Chapter 9 – Love in the Fire	122
Chapter 10 – God is Love	132
Chapter 11 – Sweet Victory	144
Chapter 12 – God Our Healer	153
A Word from the Authors	168
Connect With Us	171

Foreword

I've known Jill and Jim for more than 10 years, and I have personally observed their genuine faith in Jesus and love for Him. Jill's personal relationship with Jesus gives the Holy Spirit freedom to prophetically show her events that are to come to pass in the future.

The grace that allows this spiritual gift to operate has been with Jill since childhood and remains upon her to this day. It's obvious the hand of God was upon Jill as a child, and He has always had a great purpose for her experiences—a message for the times that are now upon us.

Jill's testimony is one that nearly anyone can connect with, even if their own story doesn't involve the "C" word—cancer. Although Jill refers to her battles with cancer throughout, this book leaves the reader in awe of another word that starts with a "C," the living Christ!

The gospel is good news, and it stands out as the best news when people find themselves in challenging and difficult circumstances beyond their control. This book's testimony emphasizes just how good God really is regardless of what comes our way. His character and promises remain to the end!

—Dr. David White, Senior Pastor at The Gathering Church in Moravian Falls, NC

Preface

Writing a book is not something I thought I would ever do. My mother and friends repeatedly told me I needed to put my life story in print, but I didn't listen for a long time. After being diagnosed with cancer and experiencing that incredible journey with Father, Son, and Holy Spirit, I *did* seize every moment to share the goodness of God with others. But it took a divine appointment with Jonathan Macnab to write my story. He felt God calling him to help me, and I just knew that was God's confirmation. When the Lord wants something done, he has a way of bringing all the puzzle pieces together and saying, "NOW!"

So, here is my story. It shares my journey with God, starting when I was a little girl and first heard in the Spirit, then moving on through my teen years seeing things before they happened, and leading up to the battle with cancer in my middle years. Holy Spirit opened my eyes to see God's army and showed me that every battle we go through is truly spiritual warfare! I live my life committed to showing the enemy he has no chance of getting the better of me—not one bit! Even as a teenager, the Lord showed me the power of His name. Praising His name reduces the most terrifying-looking demon to nothing, because none can stand in the presence of our Lord, Jesus Christ.

As visions and dreams increased, I stepped into the world of prophetic art and learned more and more about the tremendous power of God. So my prayer is simply this: that as you read this book you will feel the presence of the Lord so that He receives all the glory and praise!

—Mighty Blessings, Jill Falco

Chapter I

He Is With You

> "*Fear not, for I am with you; be not dismayed, for I am your God; I will strengthen you, I will help you, I will uphold you with my righteous right hand.*"
> — Isaiah 41:10

THINK OF THE LAST TIME YOU HEARD BAD NEWS. I mean the kind of news that makes you want to drop everything, crawl into bed, and just stop existing. Many of us have experienced this in some measure, and it has either scarred us forever or led us to a deeper dependence on God that has carried us ever since. As you begin this book, endeavor to keep that time fixed in your mind, remembering as best you can the things you felt, said, and believed. Much of this may be painful, but it's important to bring those things to the surface so you can engage with the truth God speaks to you through my story—and experience the restoration He longs to work in your life, as the iconic 23rd Psalm says, *"...He restores my soul"* (Psalm 23:3).

God's desire is to meet with you face-to-face and transform you so you can face every life experience with joy, enduring hope, and faithful dependence *knowing* His presence is with you and—more importantly—is enough. There is *nothing* you can face that the Almighty God can't overcome, and there is nothing that can stop Him from showering overcoming favor on any person who is willing to surrender and trust Him alone for salvation. Complete and utter dependence is the way, but the saving might of His right hand is sure in response.

★★★★★★★★★

It was just another day; I didn't know my life was going to turn upside down when I woke up that morning. My husband Jim and I showed up at the doctor's office just expecting the physician to shine some light on the odd symptoms I had been experiencing—but we weren't overly concerned. That confidence dipped slightly when the doctor quickly referred us to another doctor for further evaluation, but still, we weren't too worried.

Jim drove me to the second doctor's appointment, but I told him to just stay in the car, and I'd be out soon. It couldn't take long. When I walked into the lobby, I spotted a friend from church who was expecting a baby. I had painted her a sign earlier that month featuring the unborn baby's name, "Justice," a fact which would become very important very soon. Not long after coming in, they called me back to see the physician.

During the exam, I could see a screen above me with a picture of my insides. Surprisingly, the technician's hand started moving across the display, quickly but deliberately circling places all over my cervix and surrounding areas. I knew immediately this was *not* good, but I took a deep breath, trying not to be nervous. Lying there quietly, I remember closing my eyes and setting my mind on Romans 8:31: "...*If God is for us, who can be against us?*" If God was for me, what could possibly go wrong?

Once the screen was full of concerning circles, the

technician left, and I waited with trepidation for somebody to show up who could actually tell me something. Finally, the doctor walked in, cast a glance at the chart, and turned to me casually, saying, "You have endometrial cancer." I did a double take. If I'd only had her tone to go on, I'd have thought she'd said there was a chance of rain later that day. Then it hit me like a ton of bricks: *cancer*. She'd said the word "*cancer*," that enemy of all happiness, that dreaded thief in the night that you hope and mostly trust will never visit *your* doorstep. My heart stopped.

The doctor spoke again, "Hey, this isn't such bad news. If you're going to get cancer, this is a good one to get." Maybe she was trying to comfort me, but I can tell you this: it did *not* help. The statement didn't even make any sense to me. The words "good" and "cancer" just do not go together. My eyes began to burn, and tears welled up in them like a raging flood behind a dam, ready to burst forth at any minute. If I'm honest, I felt betrayed. I thought, "God, you know how much I love you. Why would you let this happen to me?"

It was too much to process at once. I called Jim, but I couldn't bring myself to explain it all, so I just told him to come inside and see me. When he came in, I broke the news. He held me close, trying to comfort me with his presence but knowing there was nothing he could say that would solve this, nothing that could take any of it away. I just sank into his arms and let the tears come silently; I was trying my best to hold it together since we were in a doctor's office.

To make matters worse, the staff then informed us we had to wait out in the lobby for an appointment to be made with an oncologist/surgeon. I was thinking, "*Really? You can't just give us a moment to deal with this privately? Can't we go sit in an empty room somewhere?*" We didn't have a choice, so we quickly looked for a place in the lobby that was as private as possible to process all this. I walked out in shock, dumbfounded. I felt like I needed a drink of water—like I might pass out at any second.

As we sat down, I started crying in earnest. My first real response to the shock came as a deep sense of denial. I kept thinking, "there is *no way* I have cancer, surely." The next several minutes were spent muttering, "I rebuke cancer in the name of Jesus," over and over again. After doing that for a while, I looked up for a moment and caught a glimpse of the young lady from church walking out from her appointment. She encouraged us and said she would begin interceding for us. Then later it hit me: *justice*. That was why God had led me to paint that sign for her baby and brought her here on the same day at the same time as me. Before all of this was over, God was going to give me justice.

Suddenly, I felt compelled to look at the exam results and pay attention to the word "endometrial." I heard the Spirit say "look again," and four words jumped right out at me "end of my trial." I realized that the first part of "endometrial" was "end," the last word was "trial," and in between, it was "oh, me" so I just knew in my heart that while I might struggle, this trial would end. There would be victory; I would have justice! I knew it, but I had to keep telling myself that often afterwards to get it grounded in my heart.

The Lord brought to my mind the life of King David, how he was far from perfect, but God *had* him, as the Psalm says, *"The Lord is my strength and my song. He has become my salvation"* (Psalm 118:14). There was nothing that could snatch David out of God's hands. Then the Lord reminded me of King Jehoshaphat, how he was facing the joint forces of Israel's neighboring nations Ammon and Moab, feeling surrounded, and instead of panicking, he worshipped God in the midst of everything. When God brought that Scripture passage to me from 2 Chronicles 20, I realized I just needed to worship. That would show my enemies! God is King, and He is worthy of my worship no matter what they do to me.

✶ ✶ ✶ ✶ ✶ ✶ ✶ ✶ ✶

When I walked out of that doctor's office, I knew God was with me. I was confident the Holy Spirit had spoken to me to comfort me, and He would continue to speak to me along the way. However, I had no idea what it was going to feel like waking up with cancer. I didn't understand how strong the grasp of fear could become as it reached for me during every spare moment, clutching at me with greedy fingers. Now, I had to come to grips with the "reality" of cancer each day, all while trying to have faith that God would heal me, which meant I really didn't want to "own" the idea of cancer at all. It was a difficult tightrope to walk.

Once we were home, I remember just crashing into bed. It was the beginning of a pretty deep funk for me. Jim was trying hard and saying all the right things, but his eyes told me how worried he really was. The day after we got the news, we shared it with the rest of the family. That wasn't fun, but it was important, because we needed to get them praying—them and our church family. It was Friday at the time, and I remember wanting so badly for it to be Sunday. I just wanted to get to church and have prayer with others. I needed the strength of the Body of Christ.

The next day, only two days after hearing about the cancer, I realized I had to get out of my own head and fix my eyes on Jesus. People had been saying encouraging things to me those first couple of days, but I hadn't been able to receive them. My weak heart and soul just couldn't get there. But God got my attention, and by His grace, I was able to get into a quiet place and just spend time with my Beloved Jesus and His Word. That's one of the most critical things I experienced during this time, the reality of our deep need for abiding in Christ. I *needed* Jesus. As the song says, "In Christ alone, all hope is found..." As it turned out, however, one way I would find Jesus was in His people.

At last, Sunday came. As we pulled up to the church building, I remember telling Jim I believed the Spirit was speaking to me about painting during the worship service. However, I didn't have my paint supplies with me, and I did not feel led to paint anything particular. Still, I felt like there was a painting of some kind in store for us. God didn't wait long to help us understand, as the moment we walked in, we saw another artist there setting up her easel. Knowing God well enough to know He was up to something, I went over to her, introduced myself, and asked if she needed anything. We became fast friends and still are to this day.

The amazing thing was what came to light as we talked that first time. My new friend had painted a very simple painting of a cross with the word "COME" written in capital letters underneath it. What a good God we have! She said she had never written a word on a painting before, but there it was—just for me. Once again, Holy Spirit was speaking to me. He was confirming I was hearing clearly, reminding me to lay all my concerns at the foot of the cross. It was a jaw-dropping confirmation of what God had begun speaking to me through my time alone in the Word the day before as He called my eyes back to Jesus and His finished work.

After we had our artist fellowship moment, God ministered to me through the rest of our church family, and I understood better than I ever had just how important they were to us. We were so loved on and covered in prayer that it filled our hearts to overflowing. You should never underestimate the power of prayer from the Body of Christ, and you don't really understand its incredible strength until you are on the receiving end of it! By the time I walked out of the church doors that day, my faith was full to bursting. I could *feel* their prayers silencing the enemy.

That first weekend after receiving the cancer diagnosis really was a beautiful microcosm of the whole journey. God showed me first and foremost that *He was with me.* He made it clear He would speak to me in ways I could understand at special moments I needed it most to lift my spirits. And He demonstrated to me just how desperately I would need to cling to Jesus and how critical the encouragement of His people would be along the way. With all of that in place, I couldn't fail—not for long. I was more than a conqueror through Him who loved me!

Chapter 2

Who Fights My Battles?

"...Thus says the Lord to you, 'Do not be afraid and do not be dismayed at this great horde, for the battle is not yours but God's.'"
— 2 Chronicles 20:15

WHAT ARE YOU FACING TODAY? What enemies surround you when you wake up, bombarding you with thoughts of fear, despair, and hopelessness? Do you have cancer? Is your marriage falling apart? Are there people and circumstances in your life that desperately need to change, *today*, or it could all be over for you? Gather up those things you fear most and bring them face to face with Scripture as we explore a passage together.

After this the Moabites and Ammonites, and with them some of the Meunites, came against Jehoshaphat for battle. Some men came and told Jehoshaphat, "A great multitude is coming against you from Edom, from beyond the sea; and, behold, they are in Hazazon-tamar" (that is, Engedi). Then Jehoshaphat was afraid and set his face to seek the Lord, and proclaimed a fast throughout all Judah. And Judah assembled to seek help from the Lord; from all the cities of Judah they came to seek the Lord. (2 Chronicles 20:1-4)

King Jehoshaphat was someone who worshiped God. He considered himself on God's side, so he doubtless expected God's favor on his life. In fact, he was the king of Israel, and God had made significant promises to the nation concerning protection and provision, which meant Jehoshaphat had reason to believe God was on *his* side too. However, Jehoshaphat did *not* know when he woke up the morning recorded in this passage that multiple rival nations would come together at his doorstep as a massive, united army that vastly outnumbered his own. He hadn't been ready for that kind of news, and it scared him—servant of God or not.

Listen, if you've been faced with some terrifying news that blew your mind and made you wonder how on earth God could be on your side, then keep reading; you're in good company. I've been there, Jehoshaphat has been there, and brethren across the ages have been there long before you—and *won*. This should give us tremendous confidence, but if you find yourself shaking in your boots, *you're normal*. Your spirit may be willing, but your flesh is weak, just as Jesus said it would be (Matt. 26:41). Looking at the armies surrounding his people, Jehoshaphat was afraid too.

So what did he do about it? The Word says the king "set his face to seek the Lord." He made a decision. He would look to God for help, and he'd look nowhere else. Jehoshaphat fixed his gaze on his covenant partner—the One who had promised to walk with His people—and he expected help to come. With this in mind, ask yourself, have you set your face to seek the Lord? Are your days spent directing your gaze to the only One who could do anything about your difficulty? Or do you mostly struggle on alone, trying your best to solve your problems yourself while giving occasional lip service to God?

I can tell you that I could receive no peace about my cancer diagnosis until I pressed into the presence of my Beloved and King, physically alone, with eyes for Him alone. And if the troubles of life are too distracting for you to do the same, and your own desires keep getting in the way of your pursuit of God, then turn it up a notch. Jehoshaphat fasted, something that Jesus later shared with His disciples was key to overcoming particularly stubborn enemies (Matt. 17:21). If Jesus says fasting helps conquer the kingdom of darkness, then we'd better listen, don't you think?

Now, if you do seek the Lord with all your heart about what you're facing, the next question is—do you do it alone? Notice, Jehoshaphat did not just set his face to seek God. No, he then called on all his people to join him in the effort. He knew that their agreement in prayer meant everything to the Lord. So who are your people? Do you have people of God around you that you can ask to join you in seeking His face for the overcoming of your trials? If you don't, then please remember the devil is roaming about like a roaring lion looking for someone to devour, and like a lion he looks for prey that wanders alone, defenseless.

It is in traveling with the herd that animals find protection from their enemies, and so it is with us—the sheep of God's pasture. Jesus adopted us into His family for a reason, and He has created us as parts of His indivisible Body for a reason. We need one another. The agreement found in the prayers of the saints can change the world, as Jesus promised, *"...if two of you agree on earth about anything they ask, it will be done for them by my Father in heaven"* (Matt. 18:19). So find your tribe, wherever you are. If the road is long and difficult to find them, you must trust your God's character, that He is a good enough Shepherd to lead you to what you need. He will not forsake you. If you keep finding brethren that you can't seem to stay with, then look at yourself rather than at them. Perhaps the wounds and deceitfulness of your heart are keeping you from true fellowship. I can tell you I desperately needed the strength of brothers and sisters in Christ to overcome my struggle against the overwhelming fear of cancer. I needed their prayers, yes, but I also needed to see the love of Christ through them towards me. As the Scriptures say, *"no one has ever seen God; if we love one another, God abides in us and his love is perfected in us"*

(1 John 4:12). We get to experience the tangible presence of Christ on earth through His Body's love.

✹ ✹ ✹ ✹ ✹ ✹ ✹ ✹ ✹

Returning to the passage, we find that once Jehoshaphat calls all the people together, he leads the time of intercession, saying:

O Lord, God of our fathers, are you not God in heaven? You rule over all the kingdoms of the nations. In your hand are power and might, so that none is able to withstand you. Did you not, our God, drive out the inhabitants of this land before your people Israel, and give it forever to the descendants of Abraham your friend? And they have lived in it and have built for you in it a sanctuary for your name, saying, "If disaster comes upon us, the sword, judgment, or pestilence, or famine, we will stand before this house and before you—for your name is in this house—and cry out to you in our affliction, and you will hear and save"... we are powerless against this great horde that is coming against us. We do not know what to do, but our eyes are on you. (2 Chron. 20:6-9, 12b)

What a perfect expression of the utter dependency of

the Christian life. If every one of us would live every day with our gaze fixed above and those words on our lips and in our hearts, "we do not know what to do, but our eyes are on You [Lord]," then we might see the world transformed for Christ in our generation. The king ended his prayer with those words knowing that if God didn't come through then there would be no tomorrow. But how did he start? I think I would have asked God to do specific things to the enemies bearing down upon me. My prayers probably would have focused on my personal desires like the safety of my family. And we can't assume those things weren't on Jehoshaphat's mind or in his heart, but we can look at his words and see the tremendous fruit they bore afterwards.

His prayers at this critical moment were focused on praising His God. He recognized their only hope was God, because God alone was great, powerful, and worthy of praise. He knew if God could see His servants' faith in Him, there was nothing that could stop Him from coming to their rescue. God *always* proves His character. When we proclaim His character, giving Him the honor and glory due His name, it blesses Him and calls Him to action while also lifting our spirits, because faith comes by hearing the Word of God (Rom. 10:17). Proclaiming

God's praises doesn't just move Him, it *gives us faith*. Praise doesn't stop with God's character, either. As Jehoshaphat's prayer went from God's power to His mighty deeds, so we must remember the things God has already done in our lives (and if we can't, we must ask our brethren and hear what He's done for them).

The king's prayer then moved beyond God's praises to His promises and their covenant agreement. Israel was due to receive the promises of continual blessing God had given to Abraham, the founder of the nation, whom God had called His *friend*. Friends look out for each other, and God is the only truly faithful friend. What's more, Israel had made a pact with God that if enemies came against the land and the people cried out to Him in faith, He would rescue and save. So what was their confidence on the eve of their nation's potential destruction? God's commitment to them. And what can give you hope today? You'd better believe it! Everyone who places their hope in Jesus Christ alone for salvation from a life of sin and eternal destruction becomes a covenant partner with God—and God always keeps His promises.

Nothing in this world can separate you from the love of God in Christ—not cancer, not failure, not broken relationships, and not even sinful selfishness (Romans

8:38-39). If you will search the Word of God for His promises to you as a member of the Body and Bride of Christ, you will find the Creator of the universe vowing to give His very self to you (John 14:23), to guard you against evil (John 17:15), to love you (John 15:9), and to pour out kindness on you forever (Eph. 2:4-7). These are just a few of the many promises flowing from the lips of our King. So search them out for yourself, hold them close, and stand on those promises in prayer, proclaiming them to God knowing He'll keep them.

When we face a trial with eyes fixed on God's character and promises, and when we choose to praise first, our praises stand as a weapon before the enemy. What God cares about is making His glory known, and what the prideful enemies of our souls hate most is God getting glory instead of them. When we proclaim God's goodness so that faith fills our hearts as we hear the Word about Him, the enemy is ruined. Satan's goal to steal God's glory and kill our hope is destroyed by praise. Fear flees in the face of it, and we live out the Word of God to the Philippians:

Only let your manner of life be worthy of the gospel of Christ, so that whether I come and see you or am absent, I may hear of you that you are standing firm in one spirit, with one mind striving side by side for the faith of the gospel, and **not frightened in anything by your opponents. This is a clear sign to them of their destruction, but of your salvation, and that from God.** (Phil. 1:27-28)

✶ ✶ ✶ ✶ ✶ ✶ ✶ ✶ ✶

Meanwhile, all Judah stood before the Lord, with their little ones, their wives, and their children. And the Spirit of the Lord came upon Jahaziel...a Levite... And he said, "Listen, all Judah and inhabitants of Jerusalem and King Jehoshaphat: Thus says the Lord to you: **Do not be afraid and do not be dismayed at this great horde, for the battle is not yours but God's.** *Tomorrow go down against them...You will not need to fight in this battle. Stand firm, hold your position, and see the salvation of the Lord on your behalf, O Judah and Jerusalem." Do not be afraid and do not be dismayed. Tomorrow go out against them, and the Lord will be with you.* (2 Chronicles 20: 13-17)

Wow. Isn't that just what you want to hear? The battle is not yours but God's. The Lord spoke that to King Jehoshaphat through a special messenger right when he needed to hear it, and He is saying the same thing to you about the greatest difficulty you face. God may not say it to you the same way, and He may not say it through a person (though He often does), but He wants to bury this truth in your heart that you might *own* it. Why? *Because He loves you*, and because He can be counted on to rescue His people. How can we be sure this promise is for us right now? If you doubt it is for you, that's completely understandable. The promise was made to Jehoshaphat and Israel at that specific point in time for that battle, and that does not mean we can take it for ourselves.

But do you understand what Christ has done for you, if you have placed your trust in Him? When you are baptized into Christ by faith, you are identified with Him. The person who lived as an enemy of God dies, and a new person rises with Christ (Rom. 6:3-11) who stands in the place of Christ before the Father. *"Our life is hidden with Christ in God"* (Col. 3:3). For any of your enemies or circumstances to get to you, they must now go through God. He is your fortress, *"the saving refuge of His anointed"* (Psalm 28:8). God has adopted you into His family by faith, and as the Word says, He is a good Father who knows how to give good things to those who ask Him

(Matt. 7:11), and no one is able to snatch you out of the Father's hand (John 10:29). Because of these amazing truths and because of the unchanging character of God, you can trust God is also saying to you the words, "Do not be afraid. The battle is not yours, but Mine."

Notice the key phrase "do not be afraid," that God repeats a few times. Why do you think He repeats it? Because they were afraid! And because it is very important. Fear is the opposite of faith, and when we are afraid, our faith in God generally fails, but the opposite is also true. When we choose to put our faith in God, fear must leave. God tells us not to fear over and over again throughout the Bible because we are weak, helpless creatures without God, and we will constantly be tempted by it. It is one of our enemy's greatest weapons. But God wants us to understand in the depths of our hearts just how worthy He is of driving out all our fears. Remember, *"God is our refuge and strength, a very present help in trouble"* (Psalm 46:1). This means we can say with the Psalmist, *"Therefore we will not fear though the earth gives way, though the mountains be moved into the heart of the sea"* (Psalm 46:2-3). When we grasp this, it gives God *such* great glory! As we saw in Philippians 1:27-28, if we don't fear, it is a *sure sign* to the enemies of the cross that they'll be destroyed. Fearlessness says to the enemy, "your day is coming soon; just you wait. **We** *win*."

When God tells Jehoshaphat and his people not to fear, He also calls them to go to battle. They can't just say they believe the Word He's given. They have to prove it by their works, as James later says in the New Testament, *"faith without works is dead"* (James 1:26). They are called to *move*, to take a step forward. They must advance on the enemy as though victory was assured, and *then* they will *see* the salvation of the Lord. This is very important to consider as we try to receive the next thing God says, "you will not have to fight this battle." How can it be that they don't have to fight the battle, but they must advance against the enemy before they'll see God save them? God rescues us *along the way*. He saves us *through* the trials. We see Him work when we are with Him on the path.

When facing trials, people typically do one of two things. They face the trial without God, ignoring His heart for them to trust it is His battle, and they fail due to their own weakness. Or, they say, "I trust God is going to deliver me," and they pray but do nothing to show they believe God will rescue. In the end, neither stance brings victory. Following God means going with Him to war and trusting that when we meet our enemies head-on, God is going to do something beyond belief to save the day. But if we don't go, we don't see it, and we often don't get saved, because guess what? **Our enemies still advance even if we don't.** So where does that leave us? Tomorrow, you need to go up against those enemies, and God will be with you. The battle is not yours, but God's.

✶ ✶ ✶ ✶ ✶ ✶ ✶ ✶ ✶

Then Jehoshaphat bowed his head with his face to the ground, and all Judah and the inhabitants of Jerusalem fell down before the Lord, worshiping the Lord. And the Levites, of the Kohathites and the Korahites, stood up to praise the Lord, the God of Israel, with a very loud voice. And they rose early in the morning and went out into the wilderness of Tekoa. And when they went out, Jehoshaphat stood and said, "Hear me, Judah and inhabitants of Jerusalem! Believe in the Lord your God, and you will be established; believe his prophets, and you will succeed." And when he had taken counsel with the people, he appointed those who were to sing to the Lord and praise him in holy attire, as they went before the army, and say, "Give thanks to the Lord, for his steadfast love endures forever." And when they began to sing and praise, the Lord set an ambush against the men of Ammon, Moab, and Mount Seir, who had come against Judah, so that they were routed...And the fear of God came on all the kingdoms of the countries when they heard that the Lord had fought against the enemies of Israel. (2 Chron. 20:18-22, 29)

The way this story ends is absolutely amazing. After King Jehoshaphat and the people heard the Word of the Lord about fighting their battles, they *actually* took Him at His Word—and soon saw His salvation! They went to bed that night preparing their hearts to face their enemies in the morning. Then, when they rose, they set God's Word before their eyes again, fixing their eyes on that hope, and they went to war! They took a real step of obedience in faith, believing God would do exactly what He said. And He did *not* disappoint.

When they got to battle, guess who was out in front? Their best warriors? No, because God had told them they would not have to fight. They believed Him, so they went into battle with the expectation that He would go before them, and they put their *singers* out in front. Yes, they took people whose only role in the fight was to praise God, and they sent them marching at the forefront because they believed their praise of God would call Him to action as He had promised, and He would vanquish their enemies Himself. As Israel once witnessed God rout the Egyptian armies with the saving might of His right hand, Jehoshaphat's army would see how *"The LORD is a man of war; the LORD is His name"* (Ex. 15:3). And they would win.

Sure enough, God proved yet again the trustworthy nature of His time-tested character, and He ambushed and scattered their enemies without trouble. They were *"routed,"* the passage says—utterly defeated—and this was *not* "hard" for Him. With a Word He created the heavens and the earth, and His Word still breaks the cedars and removes mountains from their place. So it remains to this day. When you encounter the enemy of your soul, you can trust with all your might just how much greater is He that is in you than He that is in the world! (1 John 4:4)

After all this, what was the ultimate result? The people were saved, yes, and we praise God for that, but there is more. **God was glorified.** The King of the universe was— for a moment—seen as the great Warrior and Ruler that He truly is. All the nations around who heard what God had done now feared Him, as they well should. He was standing over Israel as Sovereign Protector, and everyone now gave Him some measure of the respect He was due. This battle showcased His own glorious character in a way that nothing else could have, because He took a weak, defenseless people and single-handedly rescued them. Their inability pointed to His ability. His strength was made perfect in their weakness (2 Cor. 12:9). So it is for you. You can't face what you need to face, but *you* don't have to face it, you just have to hide in the folds of the Lord's garments as He faces the onslaught alone. You will peek out from behind His robe to let your enemies know you are watching for the victory, and you will soon see them defeated. God is ready to be glorified in your life. He is working in and through every trial to showcase the fullness of His saving might. So don't despair as the days drag on and the prayers seem unanswered. Each moment that passes only stokes the fires of His glory that will blaze forth at the opportune time.

Prayer Response

"Father, thank you for being so willing to give yourself to me. You are the King of all, and I don't deserve your attention, but by your grace, through your Son, you devote yourself to me. You defend me! I believe you are a great warrior, and I want to trust you. Please, give me the gift of faith in your Name. Make my faith in you unshakeable; make me immovable. Remove my fear and declare to all my enemies that they will soon be destroyed even as I am saved. Thank you for being willing to fight my battles. I trust you to give me victory and to glorify your Name! I trust you to keep your promises to me! To you, I commit my life, my trials, my battles, and my hope. Walk with me, Father, and be strong in my weakness. I pray in Jesus's holy Name. Amen!"

— This is an example prayer from a heart touched by God's Word in the chapter. You may pray these words just as they are or let them inspire your heart to speak your own words to God. Continue daily until He answers. —

Chapter 3

A Hidden Conflict

> "*Be sober-minded; be watchful.
> Your adversary the devil prowls around like
> a roaring lion, seeking someone to devour.*"
> — 1 Peter 5:8

SINCE I WAS A LITTLE GIRL, I'VE LOVED JESUS. I've also been keenly aware of spiritual realities for as long as I can remember. God has often granted me eyes to see and ears to hear what's happening in the spirit realm, beyond physical experience. This is not due to any significant influence from family members or growing up in a heavily spiritual culture, as one might think. No, I was actually raised Presbyterian, most branches of which wouldn't come within a mile of anything that sounded overly spiritual or out-of-the-ordinary. I learned quickly that many of my experiences would be considered contraband to the strict, no-nonsense brand of religion I knew. But God certainly wasn't afraid of such things, and He saw fit to bless a weak thing like me with an understanding of the spirit realm that many around me would never grasp. It was purely an act of grace: no charismatic/prophetic background required.

Growing up in Miami, Florida, I spent a lot of time outside soaking up the sun and playing hopscotch. It was during times like those—as I skipped along without a care in the world—that I began to hear voices. They'd come out of nowhere as though someone were right behind me, speaking. I'd look around, but no one would be there. As soon as I decided I'd really heard nothing at all, they'd sound again, mocking me, jeering like a gaggle of jealous children who wanted to steal my fun. The only thing that ever seemed to make them stop was praise. Sometimes I'd sing "Jesus Wants Me for a Sunbeam," and I'd hear nothing but silence after. I don't think I understood until many years later why my singing had such a powerful effect on enemy forces.

So I learned early in life there was something or someone out there that did not like me and wanted to take away my joy. However, this knowledge became a terribly painful secret, because I could not share my experiences lest my family or church think I was crazy. Even as a kid, I knew hearing voices wasn't your garden-variety church experience. Regardless of whether I wanted them, the experiences continued as I grew older, and they only seemed to increase in intensity and variety.

Eventually, I began to see things before they would happen, like a flash of vision as though I had lived the event in real time when I had not. One time, for example, I was driving with a friend and saw a snake cross the road. Then, moments later, a snake actually darted out in front of the car, and the friend testified they'd seen it. Another time, I saw a family member's arm fly at my face, and I reached out to catch it but my hand passed right through the image. Shortly after, sure enough, it actually happened—and it was a good thing I knew it was coming! Later in life, I was told I had a prophetic gift that functioned sort of like the watchman Ezekiel's did, as he warned God's people of what was coming ahead of time so they'd be prepared.

I didn't understand the purpose of the behind-the-scenes spiritual visions or the prophetic visions, and I had no one to share them with, but I can tell you that the spirit world became more and more real to me as time went on—and that was *not* always positive.

✶ ✶ ✶ ✶ ✶ ✶ ✶ ✶ ✶

When I was 19, we took a family trip to New Jersey to be in my cousin's wedding. It was a perfectly ordinary occasion, and I expected no extraordinary experiences beyond perhaps meeting some interesting people or tasting some potentially life-changing wedding cake. I had no idea what was coming.

One day leading up to the wedding, we took a trip out to the Maryland countryside to meet one of my cousin's soon-to-be in-laws. The area reminded me of Amish country. When we arrived, the homeowner came out and began greeting everyone, but when she came to me, something happened. She paused, eyes filling with recognition and intention (and we absolutely did not know each other) and took my hand. Then the most unexpected set of words I'd ever heard escaped her lips: "I want to take your ring and tell you about what is coming in your life." The hair on my neck stood straight up, and my quick and definite answer was, "I don't think so." She didn't seem to appreciate that, but it didn't stop her from launching into a relentless dialogue about the most outrageous things—number one being the notion that this house we were about to enter was haunted. As it would have to most Presbyterians, it sounded absurd to me.

Doing our best to forget what the woman had said, we spent some time outside enjoying the day while my 10-year-old cousin played with a friendly German shepherd. At dusk, everyone got called in to prepare for dinner. We went into the kitchen where the only light was one of those cloth-covered cords with a bulb at one end, and we hung around the table making salads and such. Suddenly, the light went off. The homeowner went over to tighten the bulb, talking to herself as she went. That set things right, and we continued on as before. However, shortly afterwards, the light went off again. The lady went to tighten the bulb again, and I could hear her say, "Oh, they want the light off."

Just then, as I looked to the side of the light, I saw a grotesque little creature standing there, probably about eight inches tall and looking ready to pounce. Before I could blink, it launched itself through the air and passed into the German shepherd, disappearing. The possessed dog then lunged straight at my cousin's face, viciously chomping at whatever it could grab, and it tore a chunk out of his nose. Blood spurted everywhere, and the room descended into chaos. Everyone was screaming; it was like a living nightmare. My aunts rushed my cousin to the hospital as fast as they could in our only vehicle, and we were all left standing there to clean up the mess in what looked like a scene from a horror movie.

With all that going on, all I could think to do was try my best to distract everyone. I looked for something lighthearted on the television, and every one of the three channels had something supernatural and weird playing. Thankfully, everybody came back after my cousin had been taken care of, but my heart sank as soon as they spoke: "There's nowhere to go, so we're staying here tonight." *What?* Stay here with the demons that turn off the lights and make dogs eat people's faces? And where, specifically, would we stay? In the *attic?* I think if it had been up to me, we would have slept outside in the car—about a mile away.

So I spent the night with a couple of my relatives trying my best to ignore everything that was happening, but the deep forgetfulness of sleep never came. I could hear one of my aunts praying the Lord's prayer, but I imagine we were *all* just sitting there praying, whatever we may have thought about God beforehand. I think we only managed to get through the night mentally because there were several of us—safety in numbers and all that. Still, I doubt anyone slept a wink. But we did survive; thank God. We made it through the night, though I'm not sure what the point was since we couldn't rest. Needless to say, we were all glad to get out of there, and nobody looked back.

So it was that I got my first major glimpse of the spiritual enemies that stalk our steps as we go about our days. It was not something I'd ever be able to forget. What made the experience all the more powerful was an event that happened years later. A relative who'd been on the trip with us that day called me to chat. After talking a while, we prayed to reaffirm her faith in Christ. As soon as she finished praying, the first thing that came out of her mouth was "did you see that demon jump into the dog that day?" I was speechless. I had carried that burden for years and never told a soul beyond my mom and sister, but all along there had been someone there right beside me with the same spiritual gift. That affirmed the experience and shined light on it at the same time.

★ ★ ★ ★ ★ ★ ★ ★

After the wild Maryland episode, we headed back to New Jersey where I hoped all would be well. When I got to my room, however, I sensed I was not alone. It felt like there was something present in the room with me—something evil. I don't know if a demon followed me from the country house or what, but that experience kept me uneasy during my time in Jersey. I was ready to leave, and I wanted to see my dad, so I decided to stop over in Jacksonville to visit him on the way back to Miami.

Jacksonville seemed nice enough, and my time there started out well as I visited with my relatives. The craziness wasn't over yet, though, as it turned out. While we were chatting, I began to hear my mother whistling for me and calling my name. Now, she was hours away in Miami, so that didn't make a bit of sense, but there it was. I could hear it as clear as I could hear my dad right next to me (he thought I was being ridiculous, by the way). I began to think I was going crazy or something was messing with my mental faculties. Either way, I was convinced I just needed to go home.

My dad arranged a train to take me home, but I immediately felt the presence of the Lord warning us it would be dangerous to get in the car. I told my dad that, and he just assumed I was being spoiled and wanted to fly home instead of taking the train. Despite my best efforts, we were soon in the car, and I was sweating bullets. I knew there was something very serious about this trip, but I didn't think I could do a thing about it.

We drove to the train station, and it was just a normal, run-of-the-mill ride for a few minutes aside from my labored breathing. Then we came to an overpass, and our front glass suddenly shattered as a cement block crashed into the car! More blocks flew through the air aimed right at our vehicle, and through our panic and bits of flying glass we finally saw a man up above on the overpass hurling those concrete missiles down at us *on purpose*. We then looked ahead just in time to see another man with a machete blocking our path on the road. They wanted to kill us! My dad screamed like I've never heard in my life and shoved the accelerator to the floor (I don't think he worried a bit about running the bandit over). By God's grace, we survived unharmed and safely got far enough away to call the police. As far as we knew, this kind of thing wasn't even *heard of* in 1976, so it left a mark on us both for certain. When it was all over, my dad turned to look at me and said, "you are flying home."

40

Chapter 4

Don't Go to Sleep

"...we do not wrestle against flesh and blood, but against the rulers, against the authorities, against the cosmic powers over this present darkness, against the spiritual forces of evil in the heavenly places." — Ephesians 6:12

LET MY STORY GET YOUR ATTENTION. We are <u>not</u> alone in this world. *You* are not alone. God is always there, yes—and you'd better be thankful for that—but so are a host of other spiritual beings. And many of them hate you. As the Ephesians passage above mentions, there are "heavenly" places just as surely as there are "earthly" places. You and I experience the earthly realm with our five senses, but there is another spiritual realm behind the veil of sense experience that can only be "touched" by that inner part of us called our "spirit," or by the Holy Spirit who resides in all who serve Jesus. And just as we walk around in this physical world and are able to act upon it, moving and doing and affecting other people, so we can be sure that spiritual beings are "walking" around and making choices that affect the rest of us. We're spiritual beings too, but so much of the spiritual realm is often hidden to us that we tend to ignore it, acting as though it weren't there even though we know it is.

When things go wrong in the world, it's somebody's fault. Yes, it all goes back to Adam in some sense, as he was given stewardship over creation, and he chose to rebel. So, in a way, all of creation has been in rebellion since. But think for a minute. Who started that conversation in the first place? Satan. The adversary. A spiritual being with a personality as real as yours and mine had an idea, and when he acted on it, it changed Adam's life—and everybody else's.

Now, we may not have chats with serpents today, but the same beings who talked with—and *stalked*—Adam and Eve are still around today. They didn't leave. They were there tormenting people in first-century Israel when Jesus came to set the oppressed free, and they are still wreaking havoc today on unsuspecting souls. They just retreated into the shadows of the spirit realm to do their dirty work in secret, in the dark—just the way they like it. They found out that humans don't like to face what they can't see, whether it's a heavenly Father or a spiritual enemy.

But this verse above is clear. We *do not* wrestle against flesh and blood. Really? Our first thought might be something like, "maybe you don't, Paul, but I sure do! Have you met my boss?" But then we must remember that Paul wrote these verses to the Ephesian church after having been nearly driven out of Ephesus by a wild mob of flesh-and-blood people spurred on by a few plotting businessmen. And that wasn't his first rodeo by a longshot. So Paul knows well what a few humans with evil intentions can accomplish when they set their minds to it. But still, he writes, "we do not wrestle against flesh and blood." He didn't have to say it like that. He could have just said, "we wrestle with enemies in heaven and on earth" or something like that. But God's Word is clear: we wrestle with spiritual forces of evil in heavenly places. The battle is *only* with spiritual enemies.

Here's the thing: God knows and Paul knows that every one of us is going to focus on the physical realm by default, day in and day out. He knows we are going to brush up against godless doctors, rude drivers, manipulative family members, demanding bosses, jealous friends, and violent criminals. And He knows we are going to think they are the problem. But here's the problem with that: you try to solve your problems by wrestling with flesh and blood. And you lose. Right? Inevitably, in the race of life, you lose. How often do you feel like your life is full of joy, purpose, hope, and the presence of the Lord after having fought back against your spouse, coworker, or parent who wronged you? I'm guessing it isn't much. Because we do not wrestle against flesh and blood. But we *do* have to wrestle; you can bet your money on it.

Instead, we have to do what Paul said to the Corinthian church and *"not look at the things which are seen, but at the things which are not seen. For the things which are seen are temporary, but the things which are not seen are eternal"* (2 Corinthians 4:18). He was talking about setting their eyes on their future hope rather than their present suffering. But the same idea applies to the battles we face. We must not set our eyes on the temporary conflicts and seeming perpetrators that we can see visibly. In the long run, these don't mean much. It's the unseen villains that need our attention—not to be feared, but to be vanquished.

As a popular band once introduced Satan in a hit song, "Please allow me to introduce myself. I'm a man of wealth and taste. I've been around for a long, long time, and stole a million men's souls and faith." The movies were right, at least about this. There really is a criminal mastermind with a horde of henchmen behind everything going wrong with the world. They are rulers over this present darkness. They are the ones in charge of the world's system. So when you see things like bad government, abusive husbands, sex trafficking, and Nazis, you can know there is someone in charge of it all, and they don't have flesh and blood bodies. They've been around a long time, and they know what makes people tick. And lest anyone wonder, yes, *people* are still responsible for the evils in the world, but their strings are pulled by a myriad malicious puppet masters.

So, the question is, are you asleep? Are you aware of the spiritual battle raging around you every moment of every day? We must give the devil his due, as they say—and it isn't much, but it's something. We have to give him a nod, an "I see you," kind of glance. We need to acknowledge his existence and his place on the earth, *in order to defeat him and his forces*—nothing more, nothing less. We don't need to give the enemy a foothold in our lives by ascribing him power or influence he doesn't have, but we also can't be foolish enough to act as though he had none. Or we will regret it.

So our enemies are rulers over this present darkness, and darkness is just that—dark. People can't see what's really going on. But *we* are different. *"But you, brethren, are not in darkness, so that this Day should overtake you as a thief. You are all sons of light and sons of the day. We are not of the night nor of darkness. Therefore let us not sleep, as others do, but let us watch and be sober. For those who sleep, sleep at night, and those who get drunk are drunk at night. But let us who are of the day be sober, putting on the breastplate of faith and love, and as a helmet the hope of salvation"* (1 Thessalonians 5:4-8). These verses speak of remaining "awake" to the coming of Christ, rather than living like the world and the people of Noah's day, as it says, *"They ate, they drank, they married wives, and they were given in marriage, until the day that Noah entered the ark, and the flood came and destroyed them all"* (Luke 17:27).

God is speaking of a lifestyle of awareness. He called the church—and He calls us—to be constantly and consciously *aware* of eternal things, namely His imminent return. They were not to sleep, or to live as though all that mattered were the things they could see like their spouses and their food and their daily agendas. We are called to live in light of eternity, to face each day as though Jesus were right in front of us as surely as our family or our clients—and as though spiritual enemies were surrounding us on all sides. We live in a world at war. Pretending otherwise does not bring us victory. It assures defeat. The army that does not defend against attackers will lose. And the army that never advances on a clearly identified enemy will never win.

So don't go to sleep. Wake up! But how do you do that? If you are spiritually asleep, how do you rouse your slumbering soul? You pour water on it! Paul once addressed the Ephesian church, telling the men to wash their wives with the water of the Word. The Word of God can refresh us and revive us as surely as a bucket of cold water can rouse a sleeping farmhand. What's more, God Himself is called the Fountain of Living Water. Our deep need is to tap into that fountain and wash ourselves with the water of the Word. This means if we want to *stay awake*, we must *wake up*—quite literally, every day. God meets with us and speaks to us best in the quiet, and we desperately need time with Him, listening to His voice through His Word. If no other time in life is quiet, getting up before everyone else in the morning to just *be* with the Father will provide the quietness of soul we need to be washed in the Word and draw from the Fountain. Think of David's passionate love affair with God, as he once said, "*O God, my heart is steadfast; I will sing and give praise, even with my glory. Awake, lute and harp! I will awaken the dawn,*" (Psalm 108:1-2). You can just imagine David rising early to bask in God's presence until He erupts in praise and worship through song, waking up the world around him with joyful exuberance.

What did Jesus ask of His disciples? In the Garden of Gethsemane, when our Lord was on His way to unimaginable suffering, He shared his heart out of genuine weakness in the flesh. He fell on His face and cried, "*O My Father, if it is possible, let this cup pass from Me; nevertheless, not as I will, but as You will,*" (Matthew 26:39). And out of the need of His heart for deep fellowship with the Father—the only thing that would sustain Him as a man through the ultimate trial—He then called for fellowship with His brethren. He said to His disciples, *"My soul is exceedingly sorrowful, even to death. Stay here and watch with Me,"* (Matthew 26:38). He wanted their support and fellowship. But they failed to stay awake. After he had prayed a while and then found them sleeping, He asked them, *"What! Could you not watch with Me one hour?"* (Matthew 26:40). He was incredulous at their inability to stay awake long enough to just have a little bit of fellowship with Him in His suffering, as He had come down from heaven to live fully in fellowship with them, identifying completely as a weak man and soon identifying even with all of their sins on the cross.

So, please, bless our Lord and transform your own life by waking up early just to abide with Christ, just to know the Father. There, you will find the fellowship that keeps you awake and aware of God's view of reality. This way, long before you feel the physical realities of life pressing in on you for the day, you will first feel the powerful, spiritual presence of the Holy Spirit and His truth surrounding you.

Now, it is possible to regularly read the Scriptures and

"spend time" with the Father without coming away awakened to spiritual realities. And that's where the next major piece of the puzzle comes in. What does Jesus say to do when He calls His disciples to stay awake? Does He just say, "sit with me, and listen?" He does have a heart for this, as we learn from the story of Mary and Martha in the Gospels, but that's not all He says here. He said, "could you not *watch* with me one hour?" Jesus was surrounded by both physical and spiritual enemies who would soon take his life, and He was trying to meet with the Father to gird Himself for the tremendous task of taking the sins of the whole world on His own shoulders. He wanted His disciples awake, aware, and active in standing guard over his time of prayer and preparation for the ultimate sacrifice. That shouldn't have been too much to ask.

Consider what Jesus taught His disciples shortly before He made His way to the cross. They asked when He was going to come as King at the end of the age, and He shared many things before giving them a warning and a promise. He said, *"Watch therefore, for you do not know what hour your Lord is coming...Who then is a faithful and wise servant, whom his master made ruler over his household, to give them food in due season? Blessed is that servant whom his master, when he comes, will find so doing. Assuredly, I say to you that he will make him ruler over all his goods. But if that evil servant says in his heart, 'My master is delaying his coming,' and begins to beat his fellow servants, and to eat and drink with the drunkards, the master of that servant will come on a day when he is not looking for him and at an hour that he is not aware of, and will cut him in two and appoint him his portion with the hypocrites. There shall be weeping and gnashing of teeth"* (Matthew 24:42, 45-51).

Servants were expected to be at their master's beck and call, and if the master went away on business, the servant was entrusted with the care of his household. Everything the master had was in the servant's hands, and the servant knew if anything was neglected, missing, or out of place, the blame would lay at his own feet. Servants had to be ready for the master to return at any time, as when he arrived, there had better be a meal on the table, a fire in the hearth, a house swept and put in order, and a household full of people who were warm and well fed. Servanthood was familiar enough in Jesus' day that his hearers would have understood all this. So when Jesus turned their eyes towards Himself as master and warned them to *watch* not knowing when He would come, they got the message.

His disciples were to keep themselves awake, expectant

that Jesus might return at any minute, and they were called to be active in keeping His household in good order. Jesus' household would be every member of His church, adopted into the family of God, and the disciples were to be the servants over that household, caring for each and every member of Jesus' family. He was calling them to be alert to the needs of the household members and to feed them—to give them what they needed to grow and prosper, whether spiritually or otherwise. As the disciples constantly checked on the needs of all in the household and met those needs on a regular basis, they would keep themselves awake and aware of the master's soon return. It would be impossible to fall asleep on the job if they were doing the job right.

Think about times you've been incredibly tired, to the point that you could fall asleep where you're standing. When does falling asleep actually become a real threat? When you stop. If you stop thinking, stop doing, stop moving, it'll be lights out before you know it. When you take a second to sit down and rest your weary back after a strenuous day or to pause for prayer after a sleepless night, that's when you suddenly lose consciousness. But if you keep moving, keep doing, keep solving problems, you're able to stay awake to reach the next goal.

So it is in the kingdom of God. We must discipline ourselves to stay awake and on the job, so that when Jesus returns, He will find us ready, actively engaged in all that He's committed into our hands. When we wake up each day physically, we need to call on God to wake us up spiritually, soaking in His Word and listening in prayer for what He is speaking about the day and the season in which we live. We ask, "What are you doing today, Father? What are you saying to me?" We call to mind how He's been at work, give thanks, and ask what's next. We keep stepping forward on a steady path to bring the kingdom of God on earth in our inner life and in our relationships and sphere of influence. We keep moving. And we arm up for the very real battles we will doubtless face that day or in that season, expecting attack, but also expecting victory.

In Ephesians, Paul the apostle describes the great difference between living a godless life and walking with God as night and day. Once, we were stumbling about without any sense of where we were going, without any knowledge of the enemies that stalked in the darkness or the constant threat of falling from an unseen precipice. Now, we walk in the light, really *seeing* both the good kingdom of God in our midst and the clear activity of satanic forces. With that in mind, Paul urges us, "*Awake, you who sleep, arise from the dead, and Christ will give you light"* (Ephesians 5:14). Though Paul speaks elsewhere of us being rescued from the kingdom of darkness by God and delivered into the kingdom of His beloved Son—a reality done *to* us not *by* us—here he helps us understand where conscious efforts come into the picture. We must choose to awaken ourselves to the realities of the kingdom of God, and we must get up from our beds—from our places of comfort and rest—to *do* something with Him.

Jesus said about Himself, *"...the Son can do nothing of his own accord, but only what he sees the Father doing. For whatever the Father does, that the Son does likewise"* (John 5:19, ESV). Jesus was always looking to go to work with His Father, and He always expected God to have business to do. He just followed the Father around and joined in. That was what it was like to be the perfect man on earth—constant partnership with a loving, leading heavenly Father. And when we wake ourselves up to this reality and seek God in this way, Christ will shine on us, showing us where to go and what to do with our Heavenly Father.

Prayer Response

"Father, I'm thankful you bear with me. Day after day, I've lived as though we weren't in a world at war and you weren't on the throne. But you are the King and you're coming back! Please, forgive me because of Christ's finished work on my behalf. Please, awaken my soul to the reality of your return and set my eyes on heavenly things today so I am ready when you come. Open my eyes to the unseen conflict all around me, and teach me to join you in the fight. I don't want to be like those in the days of Noah that just got surprised when the flood came upon them. I want to be prepared. I want to be with you so often that I hear about what's coming before it even happens. Father, please draw me near to you and give me strength to keep my commitment to seek you. Unite us and fill me with life. I pray in Jesus's Name. Amen!"

— This is an example prayer from a heart touched by God's Word in the chapter. You may pray these words just as they are or let them inspire your heart to speak your own words to God. Continue daily until He answers. —

Chapter 5

Awakening

"It is the Spirit who gives life; the flesh is no help at all."
— John 6:63

WAKING UP ISN'T MUCH FUN. Most people would probably agree that there isn't much they enjoy less than having to rouse themselves from a good sleep. It's almost painful. Now, you may be that special person who loves to rise early and seize the day, but you probably still wouldn't appreciate getting a bucket of cold water tossed on your head while you're dreaming.

For all of us, a time comes in life where God has to douse us with some tough circumstances to wake us up spiritually. Not everyone wakes up, but that's what He's after. I discovered what this was like early on in my marriage when I was homeschooling my kids. I'd had some spiritual encounters in my younger years that gave me an inkling there was more to the battle raging around us all, but then I'd gotten on with living, and that sensitivity had faded rather than growing. But God wasn't through with me.

It started when things were going well. We were living in a log cabin on a lake just north of Raleigh, North Carolina, and Jim was running a high-end bathroom remodeling business that included a great contract with Fort Bragg. It was one of the largest Re-Bath franchise territories on the east coast, so we were doing *very* well financially. However, not all was well in paradise. It wasn't long before we got some really bad news. We received word that my dad had cancer, and that was the beginning of the bottom falling out. It felt urgent that we spend more time with him, so we made plans to sell our home and move down to where he lived in Florida—at least for a season. But no sooner did we do that then we heard someone else had cancer—Jim's father. The disease was ravaging the family. And that changed things again, because we'd thought Jim's dad was going to be fine there on the lake until he went through with plans to join other family up north. But now, we needed to sell both his home and ours to make a new life together in Florida.

Thankfully, we managed to find a really nice home in Florida that had plenty of space for Jim's dad to live with us. As closing time drew near, Jim's dad was finishing the process for cancer surgery. They'd said he likely only had two years to live, which was terrible to hear, but he genuinely seemed like he was doing well, so it was hard to believe. After a successful surgery, Jim's dad stayed in a rehabilitation facility for recovery while we finished up with property transfers. It was closing time at last, and both the house we were buying and the one we were selling were set to close in the same week. It seemed perfect. Until we got a call.

Jim was flying down to close on the new house when it came, so the nurse spoke with me. She said his dad was dehydrated, and they were concerned. I called the doctor right up to let him know Jim's dad really needed fluids quickly. But three hours later, he'd passed away. That was it, as quick as that. Life really is fleeting, and you feel it in moments like those. The worst part was that Jim wasn't there. I was going to have to break the news to him. And since I was the only one nearby, the hospital asked me to confirm his father's identity after death. That was just too much. I was beyond overwhelmed, and I knew seeing my father-in-law lying there lifeless would push me over the edge. So I asked the doctor if they could just move forward without visual confirmation; they knew who he was. The doctor agreed, and that was a little bit of God's grace in otherwise horrific circumstances.

Everything else, though, got worse. When we hadn't even had time to begin dealing with losing Jim's dad, we had a new mess with housing. We'd closed on our home, but we now had to do something with Jim's dad's house—and fast. Then it seemed like an answer came out of nowhere with a cash buyer who could close right away. But that buyer apparently realized we were between a rock and a hard place, so he took advantage of us, drastically dropping his offer. We could take it or leave it. At that point, I said, "Jim, we just need to get to Florida." My dad was still alive and dealing with cancer, and who knew how long he would have?

So we sold the Re-Bath business to some friends with an established Re-Bath business in South Carolina and headed down to Florida where we hoped to buy another franchise and get started in the St. Pete area. We ended up finding a store that sold a variety of home products and wanted to add Re-Bath, and it seemed promising, so we put everything we had into the investment. We were excited, but that didn't last long once we found out we'd be getting no business for *months*. It turns out the town had planned a construction project in that exact area where we'd purchased the business, and it was starting right as we were trying to get going. What's worse, the little business we did get was less than it ever would have been in North Carolina, because Floridians want to DIY everything. Maybe it's all that sunshine. If they did buy a tub from us, they wanted to install it themselves, etc. So the profit margin was slim. Soon enough, we were finished.

We lost it all—our home and everything but one vehicle we were allowed to keep for work. And that just destroyed Jim. He remembers looking in the mirror and feeling like his face aged before his eyes. It was all gone, all those years of long days and nights working, of investing everything he had for a reward that had seemed worth it.

And he had nothing to show for it. What's worse, he felt it was his fault.

It might have been hard to determine our next move if it wasn't for a friend offering to let us stay in their long trailer up in Louisburg, North Carolina. We definitely weren't excited about it. All I could think of was Lucille Ball and Desi Arnaz pulling their mobile home up a mountain with their little car in that movie *The Long, Long Trailer*. But we were grateful for the generosity. We needed help, and good friends were worth their weight in gold to us at that time.

We felt the proverbial cold water wash over us quickly, though, as we arrived to tick bites instead of ocean breezes. We had to mow the grass and spray insecticide right away before we even thought about settling in. We went from a nice in-ground pool in Florida to an oversized inflatable one we'd dunk the kids in just to cool them off a little bit in the summer. The transition from my dream home to a mobile home wasn't the easiest either. The floors were in bad shape, and we were used to nice bathrooms since that was our line of work. It was night and day from the lifestyle to which we'd grown accustomed. We did use some of our Re-Bath skills to remodel the bathroom and floors in the trailer, as it helped us somewhat, and we figured that was the least we could do with all that our friends were doing for us. But the place still felt like a constant reminder of all we'd lost.

Three months into this new adventure, we had a visitor. A friend from Charlotte wanted to check on us, and when they saw us and our situation, they immediately begged us to come stay with them. Now, this friend was a part of a Spirit-filled, highly prophetic church network called Morningstar, and at that time we were attending an Assembly of God congregation that sort of stood in between the faith backgrounds Jim and I had come from. He was a spirit-filled former catholic, and I was a spirit-filled presbyterian. So we would see and hear things in the Spirit at times, but we didn't know hardly anyone with the same experiences or gifts who could help foster those things in our lives. God knew that, and He was already at work fulfilling a need we didn't really know we had.

Unfortunately, Jim wasn't interested. Not this time. He was all-in on getting back what we'd lost, or at least bringing us to a place of being provided for properly. Nothing could take him from that mission. He was trying to get things going, so we'd always see him on the phone between random Re-Bath jobs; in that season, he might as well have had a cord stuck to the back of his head like they did in the Matrix. He was really just trying to figure out life, but he wasn't seeking God well in the process.

The thing was, though, I needed a friend, so I accepted the invitation to visit Charlotte. At the time, we were homeschooling the kids, and my friend called up and asked us to visit Tweetsie railroad to have some fun and get out of the trailer. Once we got on the road, though, I wasn't sure I had made the right choice. I'd been raised in flat Florida, and since childhood, I'd always gotten motion sickness; every trip inevitably led to losing my lunch. It was so bad I couldn't even swing on the playground growing up. So when we got in the car and I began to see the ground rising ahead of us, forming into mountains as we headed towards Boone, North Carolina, I knew I was in trouble. We got that cold air pumping hard, but I still couldn't even look down at the dash as we twisted and turned on the winding roads leading to Tweetsie. I could tell that *my* day at least wouldn't be fun and games.

The funny part was, the whole time my friend kept telling me, "This is where you are going to move!" I was thinking, "I couldn't even go to the store here without throwing up, and she thinks we would *move* here?" In that moment, a voice suddenly responded audibly, "NOT ANY MORE!" It was a loud, baritone voice, as though a man was right there in the car shouting in my ear. The hairs raised on the back of my neck, and I looked around quickly, wondering how on earth someone had gotten in the vehicle. As my eyes searched, they landed on a pamphlet, and I felt led to pick it up. Within about a minute, I realized I was *reading* in the car, and I wasn't sick to my stomach *at all*!

I was healed of motion sickness, and right then I knew—WE WERE MOVING THERE. Deep in my soul, I could feel my friend had heard from God on this, and somehow it would come to pass, even if I couldn't see a way. And that wasn't all that happened in the car, either. After I heard the Lord's voice, I immediately experienced symptoms of pregnancy. It was like when a woman is about to give birth, and she just *knows*. My friend said, "God is birthing something in you." Looking back, I can see what God was saying through her, but in the moment, I was like, "Yea, whatever...this is *really* CRAZY." The experience made me so uncomfortable that I stayed at the hotel while my friend took the kids to Tweetsie to have a good time. But I was thankful, because I needed time to process.

When they left the hotel, I turned my attention to

God and felt His presence overshadow me. It was tangible, palpable, the sense of a real person right there with me in the room, ministering to me. And God began to speak, saying he would cover me with the jewels of Zion. It was almost romantic, like a man lavishing praise and promises on a woman he wanted to marry. I felt like a girl blushing at receiving too much attention. It was such an experience! I didn't know how to handle it, but I knew this: He loved me.

We stayed with my friend after Tweetsie, and the next day we had plans to attend a Friday night worship event featuring Don Potter at her church. I had no idea what that was, but my friend told me they just turn the lights down and play soft music for an intimate time with the Lord. It turns out Don Potter's ministry specializes in drawing people into God's presence to receive revelation—in large part through music. So we went to the service, and it was a tremendous blessing to me, especially after the event in the hotel room where God had shown me His affection and His plans for us. But it was hard to focus on the experience, because I knew Jim was back at home in a dark place, so far from the peace and security of the moment in which I found myself.

Despite my concern for Jim, God had big plans for the

night; He was going to wake up my soul in a new way. As I watched Don singing, columns began to form around him before my open eyes. There were three of them curving upwards from the stage, coming together brick by brick, and they weren't just ordinary bricks—they were gold. Up they went until the structure towered above the audience, forming a gilded cylinder of sorts around Don, and it was filled with light. I said, "Lord, what is this I'm seeing?" He responded, "This is my Levite, whom I love." So I said, "What's a Levite?" I didn't get an immediate answer, but I asked my friend about it afterwards, and God taught me through her. She asked me to put what God said in a box for Don to read, too, so I did. Though I didn't fully understand what was going on, that night became the inauguration of a new season of prophetic vision in my adult life, where I'd have experiences at a level I hadn't known since my younger years.

★ ★ ★ ★ ★ ★ ★ ★

I called Jim the next day to check on him. Though I had come to Charlotte to just get away with the kids, I couldn't get him off my mind. Already, I'd been praying for him a lot, knowing he really needed a touch from God. When he answered, though, I could tell in his voice that I wasn't *reaching* him—not really. He might respond to what I said, but his heart was far from my words. After that, late Saturday night, my friend said, "Hey, I don't like sci-fi, but I'm supposed to take you to see the Matrix." Just like several other times that weekend, I was dumbstruck. "Why on earth would we do that then?" I asked. Her response was sure, "God told me to take you to see it so I can explain to you its biblical significance afterwards." I'm like, "Gosh, really? Okay... whatever."

It was so late by that point, we had to attend a midnight showing. And there was *no one* there but us. It was late, sure, but for a theater to be empty in big-city Charlotte at a majorly popular movie was amazing. As the film started, I settled in like anybody does for a good movie, but my friend wasn't about to just let me passively enjoy it. Right off the bat, she started with the commentary, saying, "Okay, so the red pill and the blue pill are about two realities: the reality people see with their physical eyes and the reality in the heavenly realm that usually goes unseen." And I *got* that! My whole life, I'd seen things in the Spirit, but no one around me had understood. She went on, "This guy Neo is basically the Messiah figure. He's got to figure out what it's like to have the Spirit living inside of him and understand how that changes things. And this guy Cypher is Judas who betrays the chosen one." We kept at it like that with her talking and me soaking up every word until the end of the movie. At the end, I saw how the enemy thought they'd killed Neo just like Jesus's enemies thought they'd gotten rid of him on the cross, but then the enemy starts to realize who this "chosen one" is, and there is a sort of resurrection. The once-dead Neo rises up like Jesus and suddenly can defeat the enemy with a flick of his finger. He *understands* who he is. It was in that moment that I realized who I was in Christ and the power of God and His Word!

When we got back to my friend's house, the stars were *so* bright, it was euphoric. My vision felt enhanced like God's vision of the heavens. And that was just the beginning of what that night had in store for us. We went inside, sat on the couch Indian-style across from each other, and began to pray with bibles in our laps. We sought God desperately to deliver Jim from depression as we asked for wisdom. The Lord led me to the book of Ezekiel, and as I began reading, a bright gold flash exploded on the wall to the left of our heads, and I said, "Whoa, did you see that?" She hadn't, and I couldn't believe it. It had been the size of a basketball and plenty noticeable. "It was a gold ball of light!" I said. "And it appeared right as we were reading about the four living creatures in Ezekiel."

My friend got up to go to the bathroom, and suddenly I heard what I thought was somebody singing on the CD player. That bothered me because it was *really* loud, and I thought the kids would wake up, so I jumped up and tried to figure out how to turn off the music. Then I realized I was beginning to hear more than one voice, and then it suddenly became thousands—and I knew. This was something from the heavenly realm. I was hearing voices from *heaven*. The next moment, bright, golden light surrounded me. And Jesus stood there with only a paper-thin veil between us. I was truly undone—overwhelmed beyond belief. That was the moment, too, that my friend came in. She could see the light all around me, but she couldn't see Jesus or anything else (she's called me glow-bug ever since). It was kind of like Paul's Damascus-road experience in the Bible when light suddenly shone around him as Jesus appeared, and Paul fell to the ground overwhelmed. The people with him could hear Jesus's voice but only Paul had the full vision of the Lord with sight and sound.

In the vision, Jesus looked at me, and the first thing

He did was open my mouth. He pulled out my tongue like a yard-stick—it was a wild experience—revealing black divots all over it. As soon as I saw it, I remembered my 10-year-old daughter saying, "Why are you saying bad words, Mommy? You never say bad words." Apparently they had been coming out lately. And in this moment before the Lord, I felt convicted. Jesus then replaced my tongue with a renewed one and said, "sweetness." And He took the back of His hand, laid it gently on the side of my face, and ran it down my jaw, saying, "strength." Then suddenly He put His hands right into my mouth, all the way into my head, and I could feel His hands on my mind—*remaking* me.

After that, Jesus motioned for me to get up, so I rose and went over to the other couch, laid down, and pulled the quilt over my head. My friend said she could see the light peeking through the stitches on the quilt! In that moment—within a millisecond—I was transported into the heavens. It sounds surreal, but to this day it remains the most real experience I've ever had. I was flying, and the arms of the Lord were holding me like Superman holding Lois Lane as the wind blew in my hair. That's literally what I thought as it happened, and I suddenly heard Jesus's roaring laughter. He'd heard what I was thinking and thought it was *funny*! I thought, "I just made THE LORD *laugh*. That's awesome! How wild is that?" And then I fell into a deep sleep.

When morning came, my friend's husband found me snoozing on their living room couch and tapped me to wake me up. As soon as I saw him, I said, "Oh my gosh, your eyes are *so* blue!" He just burst out laughing, because his eyes are really dark brown. But I felt drunk in the Spirit, like I'd drank so much of the living water the night before that I was intoxicated; it was exhilarating. I don't know what that vision meant exactly, but perhaps I was just seeing people the way God sees us—complete in Him. Either way, that morning I was still seeing more as God sees than as man sees.

After that, we went to church together and enjoyed a beautiful service. But as I was getting ready to leave, my friend stopped me. She said, "Wait, I think you are supposed to receive prophetic ministry." Now, I had never experienced anything like that in my life, and before the Don Potter worship service hadn't even been in churches that had done that sort of thing, so this was new. I went to wait in line at the side of the church, and suddenly a young man came to sit beside me who looked *just like* my nephew.

My jaw dropped to the floor. I couldn't stop looking at him, so I asked him his name to get past the awkwardness. He said, "Gavin Roberts," and that just about knocked me out too. My nephew's name was Robert Gavin. He had the same name as my nephew but in reverse and looked just like him but smaller in stature. So I couldn't help but tell this young man what I was seeing, and he then did the sweetest thing. He asked me for my nephew's name, wrote it in his Bible, and said, "I will always pray for him." The weirdest part was, when I looked away for a minute, I turned back to find he was gone. I wondered if I'd entertained an angel unaware (Hebrews 13:2). Soon, it was time to go up and receive a word.

I walked into the prophetic booth (having never been in one), and the three people there all jumped out of their seats shouting, "She's the one! She's the one we have been waiting for." I was freaked out, and I told them as much, saying, "What on earth are you talking about?" They asked me to sit down, and they proceeded to give me a lengthy prophetic word. They said, "You carry the balm of Gilead, and you'll walk in a healing ministry. God will keep you in a special place of childlike faith all your life. You're also a prophetic artist who will paint heaven for the Lord." That was a lot to take in, and my first thought was, "You guys are way off. No one even knows I paint." I had painted early in life when I was in school, and my mom was an artist, but there was no burning passion to do it, and I hadn't touched a brush since the first weeks of being married. Needless to say, I took it all with a grain of salt. However, God wasn't going to allow me much leeway to doubt. When I left the booth, I realized I wasn't touching the ground. I was walking on air! But when I said that to myself, I suddenly had my feet on the ground again. What an experience it was! All of this was my introduction to Morningstar ministry (the church network), and it got me ready for a whole new season of life just chock full of surprises. I was ready to live there. This was going to be FUN. Or so I thought.

Chapter 6

Becoming a Child

"Truly, I say to you, unless you turn and become like children, you will never enter the kingdom of heaven."
— Matthew 18:3 (ESV)

THINK OF THE LAST TIME YOU SAW A CHILD PLAYING. I mean *really* playing. Remember their face, the delighted expression, the obnoxiously loud laughter, the pitter-patter of little feet as they ran. What *freedom* they have, these children. Then consider yourself and the way you felt as you watched them play. Did you feel bothered, somehow, by the experience? Did their noise distract you and make you want to stop them so you could get on to more important things? Or did you appreciate the moment and enjoy the children, perhaps even wishing you could be like that?

Both responses can come from well-meaning, Christ-following adults, and both can miss the fullness of Christian experience Jesus promises to those who believe. When I see children playing as a distraction, for example, it can be because I am pursuing genuinely important things, perhaps caring for my family, working to provide, or ministering to hurting people for God's kingdom. But I am yet missing the inherent goodness and tremendous value of children being who they are, the way God made them, free and spontaneous. And even if I *do* see them and appreciate that very thing about them, my longing to be like them may betray the fact that I don't have the freedom they have. I might be wishing for such freedom of expression and joy because those things are missing in my own life, and I may have accepted that I can't have them anymore. Neither of these ditches will lead us on the narrow road to the Father's house where we will find divine fellowship.

What did Jesus say? Once, He was surrounded by people (as He often was), and His disciples came to ask Him a burning question, "Who is the greatest in the kingdom of heaven?" Jesus didn't use His prophetic powers to point to one of them (as they likely hoped) or tell them what sort of great deeds it would take to earn that position. Instead, He turned and called a child to come near. Setting this child before the men, He said one of the most profound but confounding things in human history, *"Truly, I say to you, unless you turn and become like children, you will never enter the kingdom of heaven. Whoever humbles himself like this child is the greatest in the kingdom of heaven"* (Matthew 18:3-4, ESV). Now, the disciples' chances of really grasping what the Lord said were all the worse because of their expectations. They had expected a king to come who would conquer all their earthly enemies and setup permanent reign with Israel as the foremost nation in the world, and it sounds like they also may have hoped they would be the highest-ranking officers in that new government. These were all very *adult* expectations, and while they missed God's purposes, they likely lined up with what the men had been taught.

But Jesus' words threw their expectations out of the window. This was a kingdom for *children*. Were they children? They probably bristled at the very idea. They were *men of God*; they were serious, and the kingdom of

God was serious business. Hadn't Jesus been teaching them how following Him would bring suffering, how they'd better count the costs, and how He was about His Father's business? And He was saying they needed to be like children? What did that even mean?

It's a hard thing for an adult to grasp, so Jesus helped them. He said, "whoever *humbles* himself like this child is greatest in the kingdom of heaven." Think about humility. Humility is about accepting our place in the world, not seeking to be greater than we are. Pride is the opposite of that, exemplified by Satan seeking the highest place for himself. So Jesus was saying that those who are honored the most in *His* kingdom are those who don't pursue honor for themselves—those who accept the place God appoints for them, those who receive whatever God sees fit to give them. Jesus was calling His disciples to accept the fact that they were meant to be in the place of children in His kingdom. They had a great heavenly Father, and they were the little, helpless, needy people at His feet. But that also meant they would be cared for: they would be loved and would always have what they needed.

After all, the thing perhaps most true about all children is that they are, fundamentally, *needy*. A baby born into the world can do nothing but cry and wait. Someone has to save them and meet their needs, or they will perish. Even as babies grow into toddlers and young children, at first they can do nearly nothing for themselves. They must be taught *everything*—from bringing food to their mouths to brushing teeth to tying shoes—and much of the time the adults in their lives must do those things *for* them. So to humble ourselves like children is to accept our great need for God. And in that acceptance, there is freedom.

When someone releases their grip on their own fate, choosing to be children carried along by their great Father, a weight is lifted. Life is no longer in their hands. The whole world is in *His* hands. This is how Jesus as the Son could say "my yoke is easy, and my burden is light," while spending every waking moment pouring Himself out in sacrificial service to others before bearing the whole world's sin on the cross. He invites us to live as children who know their place, the place of receiving, of depending on our Father for all things and trusting He will come through. He invites us to live with *open hands*.

Isn't that just like the children you know? Don't they live for treats? Don't they ask and ask for good things until they receive them? And they generally make no effort towards earning those things (at least when they're young), unless they are pressed. Some children lose this quality far too early from trauma, but you can only lose what's already there, and *dependency* is at the core of childhood. This can be an incredibly difficult truth to grasp for an adult who has learned to take care of "number one" because no one else will. The world and the enemy work with all their might to destroy these qualities of childlike dependency and freedom and joy, and it takes a real fight to keep or revive them. But the good news is, *"this is the victory that has overcome the world—our faith"* (1 John 5:4). By God's power through our faith, we can overcome the work of the world against us and reclaim our identity as children of God. Faith in Jesus adopts us into His family as children, and we can start over. We can be born again.

This is what was happening as God allowed some of the great difficulties I faced during the season in the long, long trailer. He worked all things together for my good as He promised (Romans 8:28), steering terrible circumstances like cancer in the family and our business failure so that it would take us somewhere better in the end. He was allowing me and Jim to become *needy* again so that we might discover the faith of children. By humbling us so that we could no longer handle our lives alone, God moved us to hand the reins to Him, and we began to receive greater things from His hands.

As God shepherded us towards greater participation in His kingdom as children, we needed spiritual rebirth. Those days with my friend at Morningstar near Charlotte were the beginning, and it was just like the Matrix, as she'd said. In the movie, everyone who takes the red pill wakes up. Suddenly, reality comes crashing in on them, and it's nothing like what they knew. They're literally born again, arising hairless and naked from a sort of amniotic sac, and at first, they can hardly speak or do anything. After this experience, Neo had to re-learn everything. He had to gain an understanding of who he was, of who his new "family" was there at the rebel compound. He had to discover the battle lines and which side was which. And then, he had to learn to fight. The entire time, he is discovering his new identity, and it is only when he finally embraces it that he is able to win the war he's born into.

As I saw visions, met with God, and experienced the Holy Spirit's varied grace through His people, I began to discover what my new life and my new identity was going to be. I began to see the war that was really raging all around me and understand my part in it. I began to know God as my heavenly Father and protector, the one on whom I could and must rely for anything and everything. And it was *glorious*. It was free; it was even fun. Just like a child, I began to have fun, enjoying God's great surprises in the Spirit while feeling as secure as Lois Lane being carried by Superman—strong as steel as he streaked across the sky.

And that was just the beginning of a long journey with my heavenly Father. It was like Jesus once said to Nathanael when the fellow was amazed at the Messiah's knowledge of him before they'd even met: *"Because I said to you, 'I saw you under the fig tree,' do you believe? You will see greater things than these!"* (John 1:50). More was coming. More *is* coming, yet today. With God, there is always more. With our Father, there is always another surprise. And in His arms, there is a safety that goes beyond cancer, a security that can't be threatened. You can have this. You can have God as Father, and you can be His child. Jesus became *us*—poor, broken, us—so that we could become Him. He became an orphan so that we could become sons and daughters. He became a pauper so that we could become royalty. Trusting His finished work by faith alone gets us everything. We get to join Him at the King's table and feast for all our days and into eternity—come what may.

✶ ✶ ✶ ✶ ✶ ✶ ✶ ✶ ✶

And that's what it's all about. We are children at the King's table, if we have been adopted into Christ. We are princes and princesses with a rich Father who is over the moon about us, who has the means to do for us more than we could imagine—and who *wants* to do it. Knowing this, we should live with confident expectation of good from God's hands and a readiness to rejoice in the good that's coming. That brings us to the other side of becoming like children to enter the kingdom of heaven. Children are needy, yes, but they are also *delightful*. And I don't mean wonderful to be around, though that is also true. Children are positively *full* of delight! That is, if no one ruins their childlike spirit, which is perhaps why Jesus was so serious in admonishing His disciples to "let the little children come to me, and do not *hinder* them." Many of us hinder children from coming to God with open hands and hearts long before they really even understand who He is.

And as for ourselves, we can come to God *like* little children, expecting to be amazed. Every day, all around the world, it's easy enough to find little boys and girls squealing with glee because they've seen or heard something new, something *wonderful*. It may be a place they've never seen, a song they've never heard, a colorful butterfly, or a particularly delicious piece of cake. To a child, delight comes easily. They open their hands and receive the new experience with a pleasure born of innocence and expectation. They haven't been around that long. They haven't "seen it all," or "been there, done that." They just know this new thing is *good*. And they let you know. They scream and shout about it. In fact, it can be incredibly difficult to get them to stop!

So can you embrace life like that? Can you wake up and see the world anew? It's difficult with the rules and responsibilities of adulthood and the habits we develop to protect ourselves and get things done as we age. BUT, I submit to you this truth—you *can*. Because those who place their faith in Christ alone for salvation become new creations. The old has gone, and behold, the new has come! Even that phrase, "behold..." speaks of the wonder of expectation and delight, of looking upon something bright and new. If you give your life to Jesus, you are *born again* to new life. You *are* a child, and all that remains is to begin living like one.

To walk in this, you'll want to cultivate a heart of *expectation*. And that begins with how you see your heavenly Father. Do you expect much from God today? Some of us coast along in life, just trying to get through the day, and we don't expect God to do much of anything interesting—at least not in *our* lives. We may pray for random needs as they arise: for sick family members, for help with difficult work situations, or for improved finances, but we aren't sure God is going to do much with any of the situations we pray about. We just hope He'll help at least a little bit. And the idea that God is a Father who is just waiting to surprise us with good gifts seems a bit far-fetched. But that just means we don't know God very well. We might know a lot about Him, but we haven't spent the time getting to know Him that we need for our hearts to be grounded and secure in Him.

So I invite you to dive deep into the Fountain of Living Water. Open your heart to God and approach the Scriptures with a new mindset that says, "this is God's Word to *me*, and He wants to speak to me right now, *today*, and each day about *His* kingdom and *my* life." God wants to reveal Himself to you, and there is *always* more to discover. It never ends. For all eternity, we will discover and celebrate the goodness of God! And your Father in heaven cares so much about gaining this intimacy with you that He sent His only son Jesus to live the life you're living, die the death you deserve, and rise again to give you a new life with *no barriers* between you and Him. God is able to love you like He loves His perfect Son, because everyone who trusts Jesus is baptized into Him, adopted into His family, and seated with Him at the Father's right hand. Jesus told His disciples, *"As the Father has loved me, so have I loved you"* (John 15:9). It's no different for you!

So do you think the Father and the Son know each other well? They've spent eternity past fellowshipping in the Spirit, and every day Jesus was on earth He sought to steal away to be alone with His father even still. And God wants that with you! Do you think Jesus had some eventful moments with God during His time on earth? Just read the Gospels! New, exciting things happened all the time. And the Father often blessed the Son in special ways that were dear to His heart. Think of when the Father asked Jesus to go be baptized in the river Jordan with John. Everyone was there to get washed for repentance, and Jesus didn't need to repent, so this might have seemed like an odd request for the Father to make of the Son. But Jesus was obedient, and God opened the heavens for Him and told *everyone* just how proud of Jesus He was and how they ought to listen to Him.

Ask yourself this: would God the Father deny Jesus anything He asked, unless it wasn't what was best? Consider how often Jesus received things from the Father—any time He needed them. When He needed a place to stay, it was provided. When He needed a ride into Jerusalem, someone gave Him a donkey. When people tried to hurt Him, He'd suddenly have an escape route. When the crowds around Him were hungry, God produced food. And every demon and sickness He faced was vanquished on the spot. But then at Gethsemane, when it was time to accept the weight of all the world's sin and be judged by God the Father, the Son wanted something the Father didn't give Him—an easier path. He said, "*O My Father, if it is possible, let this cup pass from Me; nevertheless, not as I will, but as You will*" (Matthew 26:39). But it wasn't possible. The only way God could accomplish His kingdom purposes was for Jesus to die. The only way Jesus could be an obedient Son was to face the trial. So God did not give the Son what He wanted in that moment. But it was for His good as He ultimately would fulfill His destiny and ascend to the Father's right hand to reign over a kingdom family full of sons and daughters He had saved. And it was for the good of the whole world—for you and for me. It's important to remember Gethsemane, which means there are trials we have to go through in life that God isn't going to just take away from us, but He will be *with* us, and the end will be *worth* it.

So please understand, when God says, *"...you received the Spirit of adoption by whom we cry out, 'Abba, Father'"* (Romans 8:15), you can expect the kind of life and relationship with the Father that Jesus had with Him during His earthly ministry. You can expect to know God deeply and experience His tremendous love poured out on you at all times because He delights in you. You can expect Him to provide for you and protect you as the best father would provide for His little ones. And you can expect amazing things to happen all around you throughout your life. What did Jesus say?

Most assuredly, I say to you, he who believes in Me, the works that I do he will do also; and greater works than these will he do, because I go to My Father. And whatever you ask the Father in My name, that I will do, that the Father may be glorified in the Son. If you ask anything in My name, I will do it. (John 14:12-14)

When Jesus chose His disciples, he wasn't choosing them for a boring life. He was choosing to adopt them into the family that rules the universe, and they were meant to be active participants in extending God's rule on earth. They would walk *with* God in the world and continue the work Jesus came to do—which means they would *see* God at work in the world around them and through them. That's what it means to be God's kids. And that means being about the Father's business along with Jesus. If you read the book of Acts, you'll notice the apostles and other early church members experienced God working many wonders, healing many people, and rescuing souls from darkness in mighty ways. And they experienced it in part because they lived with a commitment to God's own mission—to reconcile the world to Himself, to bring about the obedience of faith for the sake of His name among all the nations. If we are willing to embrace God as Father and know Him deeply as a friend, what we will find is that He shares with us what He cares about, and what He cares about is building a kingdom full of more sons and daughters who are just like Him. So if you want to see greater things in life, humble yourself like a child, go deep with your Father, and go on mission with Jesus to seek and save the lost. You will discover life is an adventure just chock full of surprises as you walk with God like Jesus did, and you'll stand amazed. You'll hear from the Father about what's next, and you'll step with Him into it as a child, partner, and friend.

Prayer Response

"Father, I need you. Every hour I need you. I'm completely incapable of living life on my own, and you are my only hope. You're my Father, and you said I received the spirit of adoption through Jesus, so I could cry 'Abba, Daddy.' So I cry to you now, trusting you hear me. I want to become like a child in spirit so I can see you come through for me and really work in the world around me. Please give me a childlike spirit. Enable me to humble myself so I can really enter the kingdom in fullness. Put to death everything in me that is too 'mature' in the ways of the world to enter your presence with a childlike spirit. Grant me the grace to become expectant for you to do wondrous things. Surprise me, Lord, tomorrow and the next day. I pray in Jesus's holy Name. Amen!"

— This is an example prayer from a heart touched by God's Word in the chapter. You may pray these words just as they are or let them inspire your heart to speak your own words to God. Continue daily until He answers. —

Chapter 7

Fight Song

"Then the Lord opened the eyes of the young man, and he saw. And behold, the mountain was full of horses and chariots of fire all around Elisha." — 2 Kings 6:17

I MAY HAVE BEEN ON CLOUD NINE in Charlotte, but Jim was in the valley back home. He'd been drowning in depression while working as hard as he could to make a way for us out of the pit into which we'd stumbled. And he wasn't making headway. That was easy enough to tell from our phone calls, but my spirit was heavy for him too. So as we drove back to Burlington to meet him and head back "home" to the trailer, I knew this was going to be a fight.

When he picked me and the kids up, he tried to be civil and acknowledge us, but it wasn't really him. He's an Italian, and he's typically *very* expressive, but it just wasn't there. I would look at him, trying my best to *find* him—to connect with him—but his eyes were dark. Nobody was home. We drove back to Louisburg together as a family, and he quickly noticed something was different. I was riding in the passenger seat holding a notebook, and I was *writing*. I wasn't green and complaining, either. He'd never seen that before! I did this throughout the trip, as God was showing me things and speaking to me while we were in the car. I saw license plates and heard God's messages there; I saw a steakhouse billboard light up with my nephew's name wreathed in fire, and God told me he would be a fire in the state of Florida. Things like that kept happening. My spiritual senses were just heightened. I'd never experienced anything like it before.

Then we got to the trailer. And it started to rain. The craziest part was, the kids were also affected by what the Spirit was doing, so all of us were as high as kites on the Lord's wonders. They kept talking about things they saw in the spirit, and when we got to the trailer, one of them started doing a sort of Indian war dance, then the other jumped into the pool saying they were being baptized. It was WILD. Jim thought we were delusional! As rain drops began to fall, the Lord said to me, "I'm cleansing everything. Your life, your family, *everything*." And it rained for three days straight—breaking records for the area and swelling the creek until it rose right up to the trailer. We had crawfish on our steps! It REALLY flooded.

That week was amazing, and God showed us His love often, many times through the kids. One day, my 10-year-old daughter brought us rocks shaped perfectly like hearts, and she said, "This heart is Mommy, and this one is you Daddy, and this one is Jesus, and this one goes inside this one, and it makes this heart new like a birthday." Now that was special! My little girl had been able to see things in the spirit since she was three just as I had, so this wasn't the first time she'd had a spiritual experience, but the blessing seemed increased at this time. I knew God was reaching out to us, but Jim seemed closed off to the pursuit.

As God showed us things and filled us with joy in the Spirit, Jim felt more and more disconnected from the family, because he wasn't close with God. He got pretty depressed. One night, he went out, bought some alcohol, and shut himself in the bedroom with rock music playing. That wasn't normal at all, and I felt really uneasy. That same day, the first bright day since all the rain, I'd had a sort of forewarning that something big was coming—a big conflict. I kept hearing the fight song of the U.S. Marines, and when I looked up, I saw God's armies filling the sky as far as you could see. It was like what the Bible says Elisha saw in 2 Kings when he was surrounded by the Syrian armies, as God revealed how much greater were His forces than the enemy's. I didn't know what this meant when I saw it, but once Jim shut himself in with the loud music that night, I knew trouble was brewing. Then a friend of Jim's called the phone out of the blue, saying, "What is going on? God has me on my knees for Jim!" I just said, "We need prayer. We are desperate!" So they committed to interceding for us, and I felt some assurance in that, knowing God would be at work.

I didn't stay comforted for long, though, as I suddenly lost my breath and couldn't get it back. My chest heaved as

I gasped for air, and I felt like I was going to black out. Then, right before I passed out, I was able to breathe again. I was pretty sure I was having an asthma attack, but I'd *never* had asthma. It was scary, and I naturally tried to rationalize and explain it away. But just as I did, the Lord spoke aloud, saying, "I am waiting with great anticipation." When I heard that, I just knew I had to go into that bedroom. God was telling me He had me in His hands, and I could go in there without fear. I could be expectant, because He was working, and something good was going to happen.

So I responded. I immediately got up and walked into the bedroom. Jim was in the middle of listening to a rock song, but as the door swung open, the music instantly changed. Suddenly, we heard Carly Simon belting out "an-ti-ci-pa-tiooon!" Jim's face said it all. He was thinking, "What on earth was that?" But I knew what was going on. God was saying, "I've got this." So I walked past Jim with a little more boldness to take a shower, and I was able to do that with my heart in a good place and my spirit quiet as I trusted the Lord. After that, I went to bed, and it wasn't ten minutes before Jim spoke—but it wasn't what I'd hoped to hear. His words tumbled out like weights falling to the floor, "I need to ask you for a divorce."

No. That was all that went through my mind. No, this wasn't happening—not to me. He went on, "You just need to go live with your mom. I've ruined your life, the kid's lives—everything." As he spoke, I heard an intense banging on the outside of the trailer, like the walls were getting barraged with huge hail or something. And when I looked outside, I saw lights flashing by and realized there were angels fighting! Spiritual forces were facing off all around the trailer. Huge angels from heaven flew with burning coals in their hands, and when the enemy tried to advance, the angels pushed them right back. God's armies had been released to go to battle for us!

I felt boldness flare up within me like a fire, and I responded to Jim. "You are asking *me* for a divorce? No, no, I don't think so! Because *my* husband is crazy about me. I don't know who you are right now, but you are NOT getting my permission to do that." But he just said it again. And my resolve weakened a little. I could feel the asthma attack sensation coming on again, and that tempted me to panic, but deep down I was calm in spirit because of what God had shown me beforehand. So I knew I was getting hit hard by enemy forces. This was a spiritual attack, and Jim was losing, but I wasn't about to—God was on my side.

Then, I got a mental image of me lying on the floor, and I suddenly passed out.

When I came to, Jim was holding me. He spoke, "Just get me to your friend's house. The one in Charlotte." He told me later that when he saw me passed out on the floor, God told him, "this is your life without her." And that got his attention. He couldn't go through with the divorce path. But he knew he needed help. So we went. We took everything we had, planning on living with our friends until we figured out what was next. We had no idea it would end up being the next seven months. It was a time of tremendous growth. Jim and I dug in and invested in my friend's home group, exploring the Word with them and trying to develop relationships.

God just kept on doing special things, and I shared some of them with the group, but it was so much that you could tell even they didn't take me quite seriously enough. But God helped me understand that even when His people didn't get us, He *always* had our back. At one point, He proved it! I shared a dream I'd had of the group where we were all sitting on the couch when suddenly birds flew in from the fireplace. That sounded a little wild, but then right as I was telling everyone, *it happened!* Down to the last detail, it was as I'd said: birds flew in, the cats went crazy, and everybody started screaming. Needless to say, the group paid attention after that. They trusted that I was really hearing from God. He had my back. And He always would.

Now, this whole time in Charlotte was also about Jim—perhaps more than me. He was the one who said we needed to go be there, because he'd had such trouble when we were on our own. So he tried hard to be his old, cheerful self, but he was struggling. One day, he had an argument with my friend we were staying with. She said some things about how important it was that we were there and what God was doing with us, and it just ticked him off that day. He stormed out on the deck, and oddly enough I was aware of all this but unable to engage, because I was falling into a sort of trance—almost asleep, but not quite. As I lost consciousness, I dreamed of a feast in heaven. The Lord and I both had place settings, so I asked if Jim was going to come to the table with us, then right afterwards food appeared on the table for him as well, and he walked into the room to join us. As that happened, my eyes snapped open, and Jim walked back into the house. As he did, I could see it—his spirit was back! I looked into his eyes, and he was *all there*. There was light in his gaze; he was with us again. The Spirit had come upon him, and he'd been restored! He came and lay on the couch near me, and we just wept. Healing happened in that moment. It was a process, but God was working, and we were moving forward on the journey.

Chapter 8

Never Back Down

"Therefore, submit to God. Resist the devil, and he will flee from you." — James 4:7

IS THE ENEMY GIVING YOU TROUBLE? We go through a lot of things in life, and not everything is an attack from Satan. But sometimes, that's *exactly* what's going on—and no other logical explanation is going to make the situation make sense. It's important for us to learn to recognize these attacks and respond with faith. It's also important for us to enter these conflicts armed so that we can do more than just *survive*—we can win.

We have to remember how the Word says, *"Be sober, be vigilant; because your adversary the devil walks about like a roaring lion, seeking whom he may devour"* (1 Peter 5:8). Satan is roaming the earth looking for somebody's life to ruin. It's just like what the Bible said happened in the days of Job. Satan was going to and fro on the earth looking for trouble, and he ended up finding and attacking Job. Satan is our adversary, the one who stands against us. He's public enemy number one. And he has help. There's a reason everywhere Jesus went He had to cast demons out of someone. Many angels (now demons) followed after Satan when he rebelled against God, and they've banded together to destroy everyone made in God's image since.

But go back to this Scripture, and let the words sink in. The devil is roaming about like a "roaring" lion, which means he's trying to intimidate. Now, I'm not saying Satan has no bite. He can bring real trouble to the Christian life, but his bark is worse than his bite. That's one reason Jesus could say, *"And do not fear those who kill the body but cannot kill the soul. But rather fear Him who is able to destroy both soul and body in hell*" (Matthew 10:28). And let's go on from there in the above passage. Satan is "*seeking* whom he *may* devour," which means he can't devour everybody. Some people, it seems, prove to be devour-proof when the adversary comes to call. This Scripture helps us begin to see that Satan is more of a would-be conqueror, one who is trying to gain territory that does not belong to him, and his victory in a given battle is far from assured.

That brings us to a far more important point. If Satan is "the ruler of this world" (John 16:11), does that mean he wins in the here and now until Jesus comes back? At that time, we know Satan's defeat is assured, as the Scriptures say he will be thrown into the lake of fire to be tormented forever for what he's done (Revelation 20:10). Thank God! But right now, the enemy seems to have quite a lot of power, enough to genuinely offer the kingdoms of the world to Jesus when tempting Him (Matthew 4:8-10). And the reality is, the world is chock-full of people obeying Satan's bidding. Jesus said the unbelieving Israelites were children of Satan who did his will (John 10:44), and they did not take THAT well, but it was the truth. The Word says all who commit sin are slaves to sin (John 8:34), and Satan is in many ways the father of sin. It's been said that a primary rule of overt Satanism is to do one's own will, and looking around at this selfish world, that means Satan has plenty of help when he wants to get something done. So when the enemy attacks, he packs a punch.

But what does the Word say for the child of God? *Resist* the devil, and he *will* FLEE from you. Now that's a promise worth claiming! Imagine Satan running for his life, scared to death. Is it hard to see that? Then picture this for a moment, *"Now I saw heaven opened, and behold, a white horse. And He who sat on him was called Faithful and True, and in righteousness He judges and makes war. His eyes were like a flame of fire, and on His head were many crowns. He had a name written that no one knew except Himself. He was clothed with a robe dipped in blood, and His name is called The Word of God. And the armies in heaven, clothed in fine linen, white and clean, followed Him on white horses. Now out of His mouth goes a sharp sword, that with it He should strike the nations. And He Himself will rule them with a rod of iron. He Himself treads the winepress of the fierceness and wrath of Almighty God. And He has on His robe and on His thigh a name written: King of kings and Lord of lords"* (Revelation 20:11-16). Understand, that same King came to live inside of you the day you trusted fully in His finished work for your salvation. And He is here now to tell Satan what to do when that fiend pays you a visit!

This same Jesus took away the enemy's greatest weapons on the hill of Golgotha 2,000 years ago—overcoming the power of sin and the grave through his sacrificial death and victorious resurrection! The Word says Jesus wiped out the list of requirements that was against us, nailing it to the cross, and in so doing, *"Having disarmed principalities and powers, He made a public spectacle of them, triumphing over them in it"* (Colossians 2:15). Jesus faced off with the hidden rulers of the world and publicly humiliated them, seizing the weapons they had long used to enslave mankind. You see, because everyone is born sinning and the law tempts us to sin, the enemy could use it to make us slaves to sin—until Jesus fulfilled the law and paid the death price for us failing to keep it. Now, the enemy can't heap guilt on us for how we've failed, tempting us to dive into a lifestyle of sin to drown our shame. At least he can't if *we* don't let him. There is no more condemnation for those who are in Christ! We're new creations in Christ (2 Corinthians 5:17)! The old sin nature is dead (Romans 6:11). Our righteousness is of Christ, not of works, lest anyone should boast (Ephesians

2:8-9). We can say, like Jesus, that the ruler of this world has no claim on us (John 14:30)! Listen to how John puts it, *"You are of God, little children, and have overcome them, because He who is in you is greater than he who is in the world"* (1 John 4:4). If you're God's kid, you WIN!

And what did Jesus say about it? *"And I also say to you that you are Peter, and on this rock I will build My church, and the gates of Hades shall not prevail against it"* (Matthew 16:18). Our conquering King said He would build a church that wouldn't be stopped by the gates of hell. Think about war for a moment. When you're on the defensive, you don't see the enemy's gates. This means Jesus's church is an *advancing* church, the kind that storms the gates of the enemy to take back what the enemy has stolen. And the enemy does not win in this story. So not only has Jesus disarmed your enemies if you are a true child of God, He has also given you a place in His Body that is storming hell on earth to win back stolen territory for the kingdom of God. You may get attacked now and then, but Satan has to flee from YOU when you trust Jesus and fight back.

So let's return to the Word. James 4:7 said to *resist* the devil, and he would flee. That was a key piece of the promise given. You could even consider the opposite of that statement as a warning, in effect: "if you let the devil have his way with you, you'll never be rid of him." We do have to fight back to see the promise fulfilled. Your enemies don't just leave because you have nice thoughts about God's promises or because they get tired of stealing your joy. Look at what Jesus had to do when dealing with the enemy.

> *Now in the synagogue there was a man who had a spirit of an unclean demon. And he cried out with a loud voice, saying, "Let us alone! What have we to do with You, Jesus of Nazareth? Did You come to destroy us? I know who You are—the Holy One of God!" But Jesus rebuked him, saying, "Be quiet, and come out of him!" And when the demon had thrown him in their midst, it came out of him and did not hurt him. Then they were all amazed and spoke among themselves, saying, "What a word this is! For with authority and power He commands the unclean spirits, and they come out."* (Luke 4:33-36).

Jesus told that demon where to go! And he didn't whisper it under his breath, though there is power in all prayer, even silent prayer—don't get me wrong. But our example here and throughout the Gospel writings is of the man Jesus speaking aloud to unseen demons and *commanding* them to do what he knows God wants done. It probably wasn't the easiest thing to watch, either. Imagine sitting in a quiet church gathering when someone gets up and starts yelling at the preacher, then the preacher thunders back at something nobody sees to tell it to *get out*. But this is our example, and both the demon and the people recognized what Jesus did had power and came from a place of authority. Our King showed our enemies who's boss, and they had to listen. And we must do the same in His name. Jesus led His disciples to do just as He did (Luke 9:1-2), and then they were called to pass on the same faith practices to everyone on earth—including us (Matthew 28:18-20).

Notice also another key lesson in Jesus's encounter with the demon-possessed person. Jesus addressed the demon when he cast it out (and He didn't need its name, etc.; chasing such knowledge only gives the enemy opportunity). He did *not* address the demon-afflicted person, even though the person was the one who outwardly appeared to be causing trouble. Our Lord recognized that the person who was misbehaving was doing so because *they* were being attacked and were too weak to defend themselves. The person causing the trouble was oppressed and needed freedom, so Jesus went on the offensive to protect the oppressed person by rebuking the enemy causing the oppression. This is fundamental to remember when we face spiritual attacks, because many attacks will come through other people causing us trouble. Sometimes, it may even be our dearest loved ones that attack us.

When Jim and I had our standoff in the long, long trailer, it felt for all the world like my husband was fighting against me and trying to destroy our marriage. But he wasn't—not really. The enemy had gotten to him when he was in a weak place and was attacking him so fiercely that Jim couldn't defend himself. That meant I had to deal with the repercussions of the battle Jim was losing, enduring his unloving words towards me. But the goal there wasn't to *defeat* Jim, whether by argument or anything else. The goal was to join with God in fighting against the enemy that was fighting Jim, and so to win the battle and set him free from oppression. So when you face your next battle with sin and your spouse or your fellow church member is ruining your day, remember who it is you are fighting against, and turn your mind and spirit towards vanquishing that foe by the authority and power of Jesus Christ in you. I'm not saying you should try to cast demons out of *everyone*. Oftentimes people are being influenced by sin and Satan but are not under demonic control—especially if they are believers in Christ filled with the Holy Spirit. I'm just saying that regardless of the level of influence the enemy wields over loved ones, the real war is with our unseen foes, and we have to take the fight to them. Our loved ones just need our prayers.

✽ ✽ ✽ ✽ ✽ ✽ ✽ ✽ ✽

So, if we set our minds to fight the good fight against Satan's forces, how do we fight well? We've already discovered that we stand up against them, acknowledging their presence and speaking aloud to them in the name of Jesus Christ, whose authority and power in us rebukes them. But we also need to understand what weapons are at our disposal. After all, entering a fight without a weapon is a sure way to lose. We can once again look to Jesus for guidance, as He is our example, that we should follow in His steps. When Jesus faced Satan head-on in Matthew 4, enduring all sorts of temptations for our sake, He demonstrated for us the power of a few key battle strategies. Let's look at the passage:

Now when the tempter came to Him, he said, "If You are the Son of God, command that these stones become bread." But He answered and said, "It is written, 'Man shall not live by bread alone, but by every word that proceeds from the mouth of God'" (Matthew 4:3-4).

Jesus had fasted/starved for 40 days, and he was *hungry*. The temptation to get instant food was a real one, and He felt it, I assure you. But Christ's response was as quick as lighting from the Word of God, and it focused on the value of the Word of God in the fight. Jesus knew He needed God's Word—His promises—more than food itself, even though Jesus really would have died if he didn't get food soon. The Word was just as valuable in preserving His life—and more so, since Jesus chose the Word over food. Throughout the encounter in this passage, with every one of the temptations Jesus faced, He used the Scriptures to defeat Satan.

This is because the Word is our *sword*. It is our primary weapon. Let's see what Paul says about it.

Finally, my brethren, be strong in the Lord and in the power of His might. Put on the whole armor of God, that you may be able to stand against the wiles of the devil. For we do not wrestle against flesh and blood, but against principalities, against powers, against the rulers of the darkness of this age, against spiritual hosts of wickedness in the heavenly places. Therefore take up the whole armor of God, that you may be able to withstand in the evil day, and having done all, to stand. Stand therefore, having girded your waist with truth, having put on the breastplate of righteousness, and having shod your feet with the preparation of the gospel of peace; above all, taking the shield of faith with which you will be able to quench all the fiery darts of the wicked one. And take the helmet of salvation, and the sword of the Spirit, which is the word of God; praying always with all prayer and supplication in the Spirit, being watchful to this end with all perseverance and supplication for all the saints. (Eph. 6:10-18).

Paul says the sword of the Spirit is the Word of God, and if we want the sort of victories Jesus had against our enemies, then we need to learn to wield the sword like He did. And one of the things Jesus did with the Word that was so simple but absolutely *critical* is this: He fought off specific attacks with the right weapons (Scripture promises). When Satan struck with a food temptation, Jesus parried with a Word of God about food and our greater need for spiritual food. We will become far more successful in fending off the enemy if we will learn to do the same, gathering promises from God's Word that deal directly with the specific lies Satan is pushing on us at a given time. And we can prepare for these fights ahead of time by paying attention to the things that tempt us most. We can then go to the Word when we are in a good place spiritually to find and study those promises we know we will need most when we are weak. As they are written on our hearts and minds, we will be ready when the battle comes next.

Now, the sword was just one key piece of a full set of battle gear mentioned here. The passage starts with an admonition for members of the church to put on the *whole* armor of God, *so that* they will be able to stand against the schemes of the devil. The message is clear: gear up if you want to win. And this isn't just any old armor. It's the armor of *God*. And I don't think Paul just means armor *from* God, which is one way to take it. If we look back to the Old Testament Scriptures Paul knew by heart, I think we'll see that Paul got this idea from God's description of

His own armor—what He personally wears to battle. Check this out:

> Then the Lord saw it, and it displeased Him that there was no justice. He saw that there was no man, and wondered that there was no intercessor; therefore His own arm brought salvation for Him; and His own righteousness, it sustained Him. For He put on righteousness as a breastplate, and a helmet of salvation on His head; He put on the garments of vengeance for clothing, and was clad with zeal as a cloak. According to their deeds, accordingly He will repay, fury to His adversaries, recompense to His enemies. (Isaiah 59:16-18).

Now I don't know about you, but that imagery scares me— and I know I'm on God's side! Imagine how His enemies must feel when He approaches them in His power and fury. When you read this passage, you have no doubt whatsoever that this God is going to defeat whoever He comes against. And He arms Himself with a breastplate of righteousness and a helmet of salvation, among other things.

So let's think about this for a moment. What if you were to go to God and seek to put on His helmet of salvation? He offers it to us. Consider the truth of salvation, the reality that God *always* wins and will win again, saving us from every trouble—along with the New Testament reality that you have already been saved from the power of sin and death by the cross. Imagine placing that truth firmly on your head to guard your mind. Do you think Satan's forces would have a hard time getting you to think evil thoughts? You can go to battle sure of certain victory—you just need your armor on. Speaking of evil thoughts, one of the primary arenas spiritual battles take place is in the mind, and God speaks to this as well. Paul says to the Corinthian church, *"For the weapons of our warfare are not carnal but mighty in God for pulling down strongholds, casting down arguments and every high thing that exalts itself against the knowledge of God, bringing every thought into captivity to the obedience of Christ"* (2 Corinthians 10:4-5). God calls people to this process of destroying strongholds in the mind, strong lies Satan builds up until they run whole nations and cultures. Those lies start as little seeds of doubt in the mind of an individual (like the serpent spoke to Adam and Eve), and it is there that we can most easily vanquish them. If we will begin the practice of taking every thought captive—of stopping evil thoughts as they enter our minds and facing them with the Word of God that shows them for the lies they are—we can destroy such strongholds before they even take root. If you feel too weak to do this, remember the promises of God: *"For God has not given us a spirit of fear, but of power and of love and of a sound mind,"* (2 Timothy 1:7), and *"the fruit of the Spirit is love, joy, peace, longsuffering, kindness, goodness, faithfulness, gentleness,* **self-control***"* (Galatians 5:22-23, emphasis mine).

And consider another mighty piece of heavenly armor: God's righteousness, His flawless, shining character that has never once done wrong for all eternity. It was manifested in Christ who loved everyone He met, serving them, blessing them, and eventually dying for them even as they cursed Him. We can put on His righteousness as a breastplate to guard our hearts against the many attacks of the enemy against our character. We may not have flawless character, but our King does, and *"you have died, and your life is hidden with Christ in God"* (Colossians 3:3). We are covered by the righteousness of Christ in spirit. Paul said, *"I have suffered the loss of all things, and count them as rubbish, that I may gain Christ and be found in Him, not having my own righteousness, which is from the law, but that which is through faith in Christ, the righteousness which is from God by faith"* (Philippians 3:8-9). Paul was like the man in the parable of the field. He gave up everything for the pearl of great price—Jesus, and a righteousness that could never fade. This righteousness is not of our own doing—it is the gift of God. And the perfect righteousness of Christ can be our perpetual garment guarding us against the flaming darts of the evil one as he tries to convince us we are not who God says we are. We can stand righteous, knowing we are on the right side and confident that every word of the enemy is a lie. We need not cower because of our worthlessness or defend ourselves with arguments about what we've done right. We can just point to Jesus and tell our enemies to deal with Him.

Along with the armor, there is also another weapon at our disposal that's not specifically mentioned in Ephesians 6, and it comes right along with the sword of the Word. It's what some have called the "weapon of praise." I remember how I would sing "Jesus wants me for a sunbeam" when I was a little girl anytime I started hearing enemy voices, and only then would they stop. Throughout my life, I've seen the tremendous power of praising God aloud in the face of the enemy. It's not just singing, necessarily, but any kind of praise—though it often looks like singing. Praise is an extension of the Word of God. What do we proclaim when we sing worship music? The unchanging truths of the Word—lyrics about God's faithfulness, provision, and victory over the enemy. We glean those truths from God's Word, and it strikes down enemy attacks in much the same way quoting Scripture can. What's more, Paul says *"faith comes by hearing, and hearing by the Word of God"* (Romans 10:17) which means faith rises up in our hearts only as we hear God's Word proclaimed. And as faith rises, fear flees! Consider Paul's admonition to the Philippian church:

> *Only let your conduct be worthy of the gospel of Christ, so that whether I come and see you or am absent, I may hear of your affairs, that you stand fast in one spirit, with one mind striving together for the faith of the gospel, and* **not in any way terrified by your adversaries, which is to them a proof of perdition, but to you of salvation, and that from God.** (Philippians 1:27-28).

He is calling the people to stand fast and do God's work *without fear*, because that fearlessness stands as a proof to the enemy that they *will* lose. When we face the enemy with faith instead of fear, the enemy knows his end is near, and he must flee. Our salvation is at hand! And we get there by the Word through speech and song. But there is something more to singing praise, as well. Something about humanity is stirred deeply by music, and throughout history, transcending cultural boundaries, there has always been in people a deep need for a battle anthem that causes courage to rise up in the face of great adversity. That's why we have a whole book of Psalms, and many of them are full of words of war. Our life is a life at war, but ours also is the victory.

Finally, notice that the Ephesians passage about armor ends everything with "praying always, with all perseverance." That's the capstone—prayer. If we walk in constant prayer, reaching out to God our salvation to wield His great power to help us, we will *always* find the victory. God's arm is not short that He cannot save, and He's too good a father to leave his children languishing in defeat when they are crying for victory. David says, *"The eyes of the Lord are on the righteous, and His ears are open to their cry. The face of the Lord is against those who do evil, to cut off the remembrance of them from the earth"* (Psalm 34:15-16). Our God is watching out for us and is ready to destroy all who come against us. And He *never* changes. His response is sure as sunrise. It simply falls to us to run to Him at all times, as the Psalms say, *"For this cause everyone who is godly shall pray to You in a time when You may be found; surely in a flood of great waters they shall not come near him. You are my hiding place; You shall preserve me from trouble; You shall surround me with songs of deliverance"* (Psalm 32:6-7). Rescue is available, and God will surround us when we call to Him.

What's more, we can call to Him not only for ourselves but also for the brethren and all who are oppressed. That's why Paul asks the Ephesian church to persevere in prayer for *all* the saints. We all need it, and those of us who learn to fight well can fight for others and help gain them victory. Think of Jesus. He came to set the oppressed free and give liberty to captives. And His disciples learned to do the same. As we wield the sword of the Word for ourselves and equip ourselves with the armor of God, fighting day in and day out for victory against our foes—we grow in strength. And before long, we will see our prayers and our Words flashing forth to strike down the enemy for our neighbors and friends. Oh how they need it! Think of what it would have done for you to have such a friend in your time of need. I did, after all. My friend from Charlotte was steeped in the Word and came to our rescue at just the right time during my greatest trials. So prepare yourself, because the battle just might be coming to you. Get yourself ready: feast on the Word, arm yourself in the full armor of God, and expect a victory. It's your heritage in Christ!

Prayer Response

"Father, you are holy. You are mighty, and your enemies will one day bow at your feet. Even now, your Son has already disarmed every force that might come against me. Please, give me the grace to live victoriously. Remove fear from my heart, commanding my spirit with authority as you did Jeremiah and Joshua in the Word. Let my fearlessness be a testimony to all the hosts of darkness that they will lose and be condemned forever. Go before me Lord as my pillar of fire by night and pillar of cloud by day, and surround me with shouts of deliverance! Teach me to wield the Sword of the Word, giving me the self-control to soak it up daily and use it at key times. Arm me up in your own mighty armor that I might be invincible and send Satan fleeing. I trust you to do all this, because of your promises. I pray in Jesus's Name. Amen!"

— This is an example prayer from a heart touched by God's Word in the chapter. You may pray these words just as they are or let them inspire your heart to speak your own words to God. Continue daily until He answers. —

Chapter 9

Love in the Fire

> "*There is no fear in love; but perfect love casts out fear, because fear involves torment. But he who fears has not been made perfect in love.*"
> — 1 John 4:18

THOSE SEVEN MONTHS WERE CRITICAL for the future that was coming. God knew we needed that time with friends to get back on our feet both spiritually and financially. There were definitely more trials after that, though, as I went with the kids to stay with my mom in Florida, and Jim committed to getting us a house no matter what it took—even living in a van for a while pursuing business opportunities. During that time, the Lord was directing our paths to the future place we were to call home—Moravian Falls, North Carolina.

God gave me dreams about being rooted in the land there where the church was that we would one day join. It was there that God intended to move us forward in our destinies by leaps and bounds. It was also there that we would face some of our greatest battles, including my battle with cancer. So it was that we ended up facing that terrible announcement, "you have endometrial cancer," while planted in that land years later with our wonderful church family from Moravian Falls. It seemed my entire life had built up to that point, and God had prepared me through many trials for the greatest one yet. Now, I knew who He was and what He could do. But it didn't make any of it easy.

After I got over my initial shock and denial of the cancer news, I began to slowly settle into a routine of running to the cross for hope—almost like coming up for air to keep from drowning. Day after day, we began to step forward on the only path that made sense—a treatment process—but I didn't like it, and I expected God to heal me. With Jim by my side, we braved one appointment after another. It's amazing how many people you have to meet once you find out you have cancer, people with all sorts of jobs that are supposed to help you. I'm not saying they don't help, but when you're trying to expect God to handle things, it doesn't help to hear everyone telling you what negative things to expect next.

I remember meeting this one woman who had something to do with chemotherapy. I listened, but I really just couldn't take in what she was saying. It wasn't something I was willing to accept. The blur of information about radiation and medicines—how this one causes nausea and that one might not, but that one might do something else terrible to you—was just too much. We walked through a room where a bunch of people were sitting, like a huge barber shop with chairs lined up all along the wall. Instead of getting haircuts, they were getting chemo! Some of these sweet souls had hair, but the rest sported a variety of bandanas and wigs.

I remember having this intense feeling of just wanting to run away. I just wanted to go back to my life from a week earlier. I couldn't accept this new reality. How did I end up in this place? Then I came crashing back into the moment with jarring finality as a woman's voice told me about the wonderful wig shop they had available. I've always had really thick hair that everybody talked about and that I loved. So this was a point of major contention for me. But I couldn't stay bothered about it long without getting convicted. Nearly immediately, I thought, "Lord, forgive me for pride about my hair!" It was a crazy moment.

While going through all those introductory steps in the treatment process, I remember feeling like I wasn't all there. It was like I was watching my life as a movie, as if I was outside of myself. I couldn't receive anything the physicians were telling me. I remember thinking, "Why are you showing me all of these things? I am not going to come here and do chemotherapy and lose my hair." Unfortunately, it's not because my faith was great. Mostly, I just had a mental wall up, but I was somewhere between being in denial and genuinely wanting to have God's heavenly perspective which might disagree with the wisdom of the world. When I got back in the car after the visit with the chemotherapy professionals, that wall began to crumble. There was a part of me that just wanted to break down and fall apart. But I remember feeling the mighty presence of the Lord's love in that moment restoring my hope and vitality. As Jim drove home, I closed my eyes while the Lord brought me back to a time that he had given me a beautiful vision, months earlier.

I was sitting in my car in the middle of a parking lot under a great oak tree, its mighty limbs stretching towards the sun above. My eyes were wide open, and I was just talking to Jesus. Looking up at the clouds, I poured out my heart to Him, telling him how I adored Him and He was my whole world. As I spoke to Him, suddenly pink mist began to form in the distance, thickening as it floated closer to me. It moved towards me with intention, almost as if in response to my words, growing as it went. The color began to shift as the pink deepened into a romantic red—somewhat like a Valentine's heart, or an anniversary rose. It stopped about 30 feet away from me, hovering there in the sky like a present waiting to be opened, and it suddenly turned into a ruby, filling my view. I said, "WOW, Lord, that is beautiful! I love you so much!" That instant a heart shot right out of the ruby and into my chest. It hit me like a waterfall of love and delight. Tears of joy streamed down my face, and my soul began to erupt in delighted laughter. I could hardly contain myself!

Driving home from the chemotherapy facility months

later with this memory in my mind, I knew the Holy Spirit was releasing His agape love to me so that I might be filled with hope despite the cancer news. It was like the Word says, *"Now may the God of hope fill you with all joy and peace in believing, that you may abound in hope by the power of the Holy Spirit"* (Romans 15:13). My whole countenance changed! The Lord was letting me know to set my eyes on heavenly things, not on the things of the earth. There was a reality that was above and beyond the reality I could see.

This ended up being very, very important for me to understand, especially as the days dragged on without me being healed. The more appointments I went to, the more I began to feel like my life was on hold until I got this behind me. I needed to get on with my life! I remember confessing to the Lord that I just *hated* all the doctor's appointments. I didn't want to be subject to what they had to say. I didn't even want to be in the atmosphere of the building! It felt like they owned me. And God's Word would convict me, saying, "count it all joy," to which I could only cry, "But how Lord? Show me how!" Then I remember hearing in the spirit, "be thankful." I began to thank Him for everything I was experiencing in life and how He was going to surely use it for His glory. I had to go to the cross again and again and lay all my cares down there before God. I told Him that I truly did believe the Word, and I truly did cast all my cares upon Him. Our Father kept reminding me through His Holy Spirit dwelling in me and through His Word that He had given me life and was not surprised by any of my tomorrows.

The idea that my story was already written really resonated with me. But I was still a little bit confused, thinking, "If my story is already written, why cancer?" And yet, I was beginning to understand that trials were ways for us to draw ever closer to God. And God knows I care about getting closer to Him; I guess I just hadn't thought I needed all the trouble to get there. But let's face it, if we didn't go through difficult things, it's just too easy to get wrapped up in everyday things and forget God. Trials put us on our faces in surrender before the Lord and cause us to dig deeper into His Word to hear from Him. That's why the Bible says, *"Therefore submit to God. Resist the devil and he will flee from you"* (James 4:7). The enemy can't steal our joy and ruin our lives if he's running from us, and that comes from submitting ourselves fully to God and His plans. It comes from surrender. All I can say is the deeper I went into God's truth and the more time I spent on my face before God, the more I understood this journey wouldn't be in vain.

There was one particular night that this revelation about the journey not being in vain became intensely personal between me and Jesus. I lay in bed in the dark looking up at the tongue and groove pine boards above me, when the room suddenly darkened until the ceiling looked like an empty void—like space. I was speaking to Jesus, not wanting to bring up my concerns all over again, because I felt like a broken record. I knew He had to be tired of hearing it all, and it hurt a little bit to tell Him knowing that meant I didn't fully trust Him, and He was *so* trustworthy. I kept putting my fears at the foot of the cross, but I only had to keep doing that so much because I hadn't learned to *leave them there* yet. All I wanted was to be in a quiet place with my Beloved, knowing I was in His arms, laying everything down again and just telling Him how much I loved Him. My favorite place was in His presence.

As I poured out my heart to Jesus, stars suddenly began to appear before my eyes, sparkling to life in the now black expanse of the ceiling. Before I knew it, the entire room was filled with them. It was like I'd sailed out into the vast sea of the universe with God. I even saw shooting stars rocket past me here and there. It was amazing. Heaven had come to earth. To this day, if I go into a quiet place with God like that, He will bring me to this place of heaven on earth. It's tremendously comforting.

Shortly after that time I first experienced the vision of the stars, I asked the Lord if He would show the same thing to another sweet couple we knew who are now good friends of ours today. And it happened! They later told us they saw the stars too as they lay in bed. But they described colors that I didn't see. When I heard that, I laughed, saying, "That was all for you! That was your own special blessing from the Lord." That was a lot of fun to discover God would do things like that. I believe He just wants us to feel blessed. And this happens when we make ourselves vulnerable, when we reveal our hearts to Him, taking the time to be in His presence in an intimate way. Giving Him all of us gets us all of Him.

Moments like these strengthened my faith and deepened my relationship with my Beloved. But the appointments kept coming, threatening to dampen my spirit. Each was like a tick of the clock counting down towards the big day—surgery day. As time went on, winter came, and it was time to get a Christmas tree. Jim and I decided we had better keep traditions going as best we could and not submit to the idea that life was on hold. So we went to pick out a live tree the day after Thanksgiving as we always had. We found the most beautifully-shaped tree, and we excitedly brought it home. But the excitement didn't last long.

We first noticed it needed a couple of limbs at the bottom cut off to fit the stand, which wasn't a big deal, so Jim got to work. He cut a lower limb off, but when it broke free, the whole lower part of the tree opened up to reveal a gnarled mess inside. It looked terrible. Still, we could just hide it, so I told Jim to prop it up against the building, and we'd decorate it anyway. But he stopped me, saying, quite seriously, "No, God just told me I have to burn it." As odd as that was, we've just learned to do whatever we hear God say, so Jim set that thing on fire. And he went right out to get another.

The one he brought back was lovely. When he cut off the lower limbs this time, the new tree did great. Once we put it up, though, things got interesting. We put it in some warm water, and it drank a ridiculous amount, considering it was without roots—something like a gallon per day from Thanksgiving through Christmas. Then, when the new year came, something absolutely amazing happened. But I'll get back to that later.

Chapter 10

God Is Love

"Beloved, let us love one another, for love is of God; and everyone who loves is born of God and knows God. He who does not love does not know God, for God is love."

— 1 John 4:7-8

DOES GOD LOVE YOU TODAY? If you hesitated *at all* in answering that, let me help you out. YES, He does! Your heavenly Father *loves* YOU. And it has nothing to do with what you've done or not done for Him. Now, for many of us, we said "yes" all too easily, but we have to pause and ask ourselves whether we meant it. We need to check our hearts in this moment to be sure they line up with our heads. Do you *feel* loved by God today? Feelings aren't everything, but our emotions often tell the story of what we really believe in our hearts. Are you plagued with anxiety, because you secretly fear God won't take care of some things in life that trouble you? Do you feel like a failure who has no value because you haven't reached your goals lately? Have you fallen into sinful life patterns, avoiding hearing from God's Word or talking to Him because you feel guilty? If you said "yes" to any of those questions, then you *are* struggling to trust God's love for you today. And that's *normal*—but you don't have to live there.

Look at the above verse from 1 John 4:7-8. See how it ends, with, *"He who does not love does not know God, for God is love."* This whole passage is about how believers will love other people because of the love they have received from God. But let's not get too hung up just now on the "us" part—the command to love others. Rather, let us pay attention to God here. What did it say? God *is* love. It didn't say, "He *has* love," "He *feels* love," or even "He *shows* love," though John could have said it one of those ways. No, God's inspiration led the apostle to say love was a piece of God's very identity. One can't *know* God without knowing love, because He is love. And the passage goes on to say, later, *"There is no fear in love, but perfect love casts out fear. For fear has to do with punishment, and whoever fears has not been perfected in love"* (1 John 4:18, ESV). So when we are filled with fear about anything at all, we can understand that this results from our lack of connection to God's love. We have not been "perfected" or "made complete" in love. You see, God's love provides for us everything our soul lacks. Truly, only to God can the iconic words, "you complete me," be honestly spoken. And when we lack, we lack because we're living on far less of God's love than we ought.

So what can be done? When we've strayed from God's love, we haven't *stayed* in God's love. Kids only feel loved by their parents if they are with their parents often, hearing the words "I love you," and seeing that love in action. So it is with God. And He calls us to abide, to stay, with Him. The 1 John passage says, *"God is love, and he who abides in love abides in God, and God in him"* (1 John 4:16b).

Staying in God's love means staying with God, and staying with God means staying in His love. It's all about presence. We need to be near God in spirit and aware of how He is working around us for our good, like kids who see their parents doing things with and for them. And that starts with invitation.

God is already inviting us near, as the Word promises, *"Draw near to God, and He will draw near to you"* (James 4:8). This invitation is a standing one that is never taken back. In fact, God sent His only son, Jesus, to make peace between Himself and us (Romans 5:1) so that we could become as close as it's possible to become—so that we could become one with Him (John 17:11). All that remains, therefore, is for us to invite God near. We can do this through prayer, the sort Paul is calling us to when he says, *"Rejoice always, pray without ceasing, in everything give thanks; for this is the will of God in Christ Jesus for you"* (1 Thess. 5:16-18). Starting with giving thanks, we can move towards a place where we nearly never stop praying—and never stop seeing God answer. This may sound like a tall order if you currently pray here or there in a quiet place for a few minutes, but God's children across the ages have discovered the deep joys of God's presence through consistent prayer. If you will begin to thank your heavenly Father for each and every good thing in your life, you'll begin to draw closer to Him as you see Him at work around you, providing for you. He already was, so it's only your awareness of it that grows. But as you become more aware of His presence, your faith will grow, leading you to ask for Him to be more involved in your life—which means you'll see *more* of His work!

Speaking of work, we can involve God in our work and become more involved in God's work. And that will draw us closer to Him! Jesus said, *"If anyone loves Me, he will keep My word; and My Father will love him, and We will come to him and make Our home with him"* (John 14:23). This promise from Jesus shows just how much God longs for closeness with us—so much that He would make us His *home*. We are where God wants to hang His hat and relax. We are the place He wants to stay. And He wants to be at home in everyone who loves Him, but this Scripture shows us that we experience His presence in and through obeying Him. Obedience is God's love language, and we show Him love by doing the things He says. It shows we trust His heart for us, knowing if He said it, it's good for us. And when we do the things He says, we experience His presence and joy as He does things *with* us. It's like Jesus said, "*Truly, truly, I say to you, the Son can do nothing of his own accord, but only what he sees the Father doing. For whatever the Father does, that the Son does likewise. For the Father loves the Son and shows him all that he himself is doing*" (John 5:19-20, ESV). This was Jesus's experience, a life full of the Father's presence as they worked together in the world, and He said the Father would love us the same way (John 15:9, 16:27). When we invite God to show us what He's doing and take part in it, we experience more of His presence and more of His love.

One of the ways God shows us what He's doing is through His Word, and as many know, communication is key for any relationship. We will experience God talking with us and hear more about His love for us and His plans for us if we regularly feast on His Word. After all, Jesus said, "*Man shall not live by bread alone, but by every word that proceeds from the mouth of God*" (Matthew 4:4). In this life, we need to hear from God as much as we need to *eat*. His Word sustains us, acting as a source of life, as Jesus said in John 6:63, "*The words that I speak to you are spirit, and they are life.*" If we struggle physically at times because of skipped meals or bad nutrition, how much more are we struggling in spirit when we decline God's invitation to feed on His Word daily? As His Word makes its way into our hearts over time, His promises come to life, and we experience life by His side more and more. The best part is, His Word is then ready in our hearts to remind us of His love any time we don't feel it, especially when we are going through hard times.

When I was walking through some of the hardest days dealing with cancer, God's love was what sustained me, and His Word was often what gave me the hope to continue. The more appointments I went to, the more desperate I would feel about my situation, but God would send a Word to help me. He would use James 1 to convict me, saying, "count it all joy when you face trials," to which I could only cry, "But how Lord? Show me how!" I remember hearing in the Spirit, "be thankful." I began to thank Him for everything I was experiencing in life and how He was going to surely use it for His glory. I had to go to the cross again and again and lay all my cares down there before God, remembering what Jesus had done for me, proving His love. It was like coming up for air to keep from drowning. I was desperate, and God's love sustained me. Knowing how much I was struggling, God even went the extra mile to show me His love, sending me a vision of a heart in the sky that shot into my chest. When that happened, the Holy Spirit released His agape love to me, like Paul prayed for the Roman church to experience, *"Now may the God of hope fill you with all joy and peace in believing, that you may abound in hope by the power of the Holy Spirit"* (Romans 15:13). The Holy Spirit fills us with hope, and *"...hope does not disappoint, because the love of God has been poured out in our hearts by the Holy Spirit who was given to us"* (Romans 5:5). God's love sustained me in my worst times, and it will sustain you, if you abide in it. It's more amazing than you could dream. God tells us what His love is like in 1 Corinthians 13:4-8:

> *Love suffers long and is kind; love does not envy; love does not parade itself, is not puffed up; does not behave rudely, does not seek its own, is not provoked, thinks no evil; does not rejoice in iniquity, but rejoices in the truth; bears all things, believes all things, hopes all things, endures all things. Love never fails.*

God's love is unending and far greater than our own. Just read through some of these verses and consider how badly your love fails to meet this standard. In Isaiah, God says something that may be familiar to many of us, *"For as the heavens are higher than the earth, so are My ways higher than your ways, and My thoughts than your thoughts"* (Isaiah 55:8-9), which helps us understand that He and His ways are *beyond* us. But we need to see what God was talking about. The verses just before that shared God's heart for His people, Israel, saying, *"Seek the Lord while He may be found, call upon Him while He is near. Let the wicked forsake his way, and the unrighteous man his thoughts; let him return to the Lord, and He will have mercy on him; and to our God, for He will abundantly pardon"* (Isaiah 55:6-7). God was ready to have mercy and forgive all of Israel's sins, even though they had denied Him and worshipped other gods for years. His love for them was so great, He felt He had to give them an astounding metaphor just to help them get it. His love was so much *more* than theirs, trying to grasp it was like standing on the ground trying to see into space. He knew they wouldn't forgive or show mercy like this, and it would be hard for them to believe His love was great enough to take them back, so He tried to help them understand and turn back to Him.

Then, as time and again the world didn't really understand God's love, God sent His Son Jesus to make it tangible, to reveal the heart of the Father. Think of what He did to show that love. He left heaven. He spent 33 years on earth in weakness, enduring splinters and sweat and stress, and He did it without once choosing Himself over another person. He sought and saved the lost. He set people free from addictions and demons and sickness. He confronted authority figures who were abusing their power at risk of his own reputation and his life. He was betrayed. He endured the unjust torture of being wrongly accused of a crime, punished, insulted, and ultimately killed. He even faced the wrath of God for all humanity's evil for all time. And He did it all for those He called His friends (John 15:13). That's what love is!

The earth is positively *full* of the steadfast love of the Lord, as the Psalms say (Psalm 33 and many others). This means you can't get away from it, no matter where you go or how far you fall. This God is *dedicated* to caring about you and me. And He is what we need when we face trials. So lean close, like John did at the last supper with Jesus, resting on Him, and invite your heavenly Father into every area of your life. Thank Him and expect Him to answer prayers and to work in the world around you. Go with Him to work like Jesus did and see all that He had planned for you since before the world existed. And when storms threaten to destroy you, *expect* His presence in them—and He will always be enough.

Prayer Response

"Father, your love is amazing. Thank you for loving me. I repent of doubting your love so often in so many circumstances. My actions betray that I haven't really trusted your commitment to me, but I want to! I dearly want to. Please shed your love abroad in my heart and through your Holy Spirit fill me with hope. Wash me in your love, drowning me in it until I can't help but pour it out on others around me. Your Son gave Himself for me, suffered for me, bled for me, and you judged Him for me. Thank you for proving your love to me so surely that I could never doubt it—even though I have doubted. I trust your love forgives me. Father, help me to abide in your love and to obey you so you know I love you back. I want to go deeper with you until we are fully one. You're my everything. You complete me. I pray in Jesus's holy Name. Amen!"

— This is an example prayer from a heart touched by God's Word in the chapter. You may pray these words just as they are or let them inspire your heart to speak your own words to God. Continue daily until He answers. —

Chapter 11

Sweet Victory

"Come and see what God has done:
he is awesome in his deeds toward the
children of man."— Psalm 66:5, ESV

THE CALL FINALLY CAME. It was time. The surgeon was ready to remove the cancer that was trying to kill me, so we finished our appointment by scheduling a day for the operation. And believe me, I wanted it gone, but surgery still wasn't an exciting prospect. To make matters worse, the doctor said, "How's December 23 for surgery?" My answer was immediate. "*No*, no way. I am *not* coming home for Christmas right after surgery. This is not going to be a Christmas memory. What do you have after the first of the year?" She looked at me like I was crazy. You could tell she thought it was absolutely nuts to postpone saving my life for the sake of not tainting a holiday memory. But she didn't know the God I knew. He had this. He could handle a few more days, and Christmas was a big deal to Him too.

Crazy or not, she respected my wishes and scheduled the operation for January 2nd. We were thankful for that for more than one reason, as we also ended up needing the procedure to happen in the new year for insurance to pay for it. The doctor kept talking me through the upcoming surgery, then she suddenly looked at me and said, "We wash glitter off of people's stomachs if they come in for surgery with glitter on them." Now, that probably doesn't make sense to anyone who doesn't know me, but there is a good reason she felt she had to say that.

Years ago, I had a family dispute that left me crying on the bathroom floor with a broken heart. When I got up, I was covered in shiny particles of some kind. I thought maybe I had bent over in some glittery lotion someone had spilled on the floor or something like that. But then, when I put my clothes on, it was all over them, and when I got in the car, it was all over the car! God revealed to me that it was His Shekinah glory. It appeared as a silver-gold sheen flecked with red and gold that covered me at times from the top of my head to the bottom of my feet. The Lord gave it to me to encourage me with His presence, and in time He used it to encourage others, as He would have me stand in the front of church services to release the glory for people during worship. It would also get all over my paintings. I believe it was released on people so that they then carried the manifest glory of God.

So when that oncologist told me I'd better be ready to have glitter washed off of me, I looked at Jim, thinking, "Oh, Lord, you are kidding me." I knew she'd seen the glory. Usually, I really had to get out in the sun for people to see it, but there it was as clear as day in blue fluorescent lighting. I didn't have much choice but to explain it as best I could, and it was a chance to testify of God's miracles. So I told her. It wasn't something that would wash off. It was a supernatural display of God's glory. I said, "Well, you can think I'm some crazy person who covers themselves in glitter, or you can think I'm some crazy person who believes God does it." I figured it was better that God got the glory, however she saw it. I went on, "When we get to surgery time, you can go ahead and wash my stomach off, but you're going to see the glitter reappear supernaturally afterwards, and if you have any clothing or a cloth or anything near me, it will appear on that too."

★ ★ ★ ★ ★ ★ ★ ★ ★ ★

January 2nd came soon enough. Jim and I got up long before dawn to get ourselves and the kids ready for surgery that morning in Winston Salem. It was an hour's drive and an early appointment. I remember asking Jim to play some worship music in the car, and I just lay back and sang all the way there. At one point during the trip, I could see Jim thinking, and he shared how well he thought I was handling all this. That was nice, but when he said it, the Lord corrected him right away. It wasn't me handling things well. It was Jesus holding me tighter and teaching me to trust by leaning deeper. It was less of me and more of Jesus. I was becoming an emptier vessel and receiving more and more of His fullness. The best part of the trip came after that, as we arrived to find an enormous star on top of the hospital building. Now we all know that was the hospital's attempt at decorating for the holidays, but I also knew Jesus was saying to me, "I'm right here." It reminded me of how God had supernaturally shown me the stars on the bedroom ceiling. He was comforting me once again.

Once there, I had to get prepped for surgery, and then it was time to go in. The hospital sent a wheelchair and an attendant to take me to the operating room. When he walked in, I just knew he was born again. He was a large African American man with the nicest smile, and he greeted me by saying, "Jill Falco, what can I do to put you at ease?" I smiled and said, half-joking, "Well, you could sing worship songs to me until we get in that operating room." He didn't bat an eye before starting up singing "How Great Is Our God" by Chris Tomlin. Joy and peace washed over me like an overwhelming stream. God was there in more ways than one. And I needed it. There I was with my little cloth shower cap on my head, vulnerable as can be, surrounded by my family who were worried about me and the constant warnings of hospital staff preparing us for the worst. They kept saying things like "you are probably going to need a blood transfusion." And I needed every reminder of hope. I kept praying, "Jesus, you always have my back. You word is true. We will always cast our cares upon you. You bore stripes for our healing and said we would see greater miracles." Then the lights went out—for me, at least.

I don't remember much from when I woke up after surgery, but everyone said it went well, so I was thankful. In the hospital room where I recovered afterwards, they had me hooked up to electrodes massaging my calves and kept telling me to blow into a tube hard enough to keep the little buoy floating properly. I kept at that most of the day with no idea what they'd found in the operating room. Then the doctor came in and just said, "You did fine. We'll let you know the results in about a week." It was a bit anticlimactic, but that time was coming. By the next day, I got to go home.

When I got there, I remember sitting in the recliner looking around at all the Christmas decorations that were going to have to come down. Thankfully, family was helping—and not just immediate family, but brothers and sisters in the Lord were coming by and bringing food and such. I felt a lot of love from everyone. Then we got around to dealing with the Christmas tree, and when we started taking off the ornaments, I saw something I couldn't believe. It was *growing*. "Jim, look at the tree!" I shouted. All over the tree, from top to bottom, little puffs of green had appeared on the tips of branches. This dead thing that had been chopped down at least two months prior and which had no roots was, somehow, *blooming!* It was all new growth. I could hardly believe my eyes. Later, my friend from church told me the two trees were prophetic signs. She said, "Jill, the trees are metaphors for what you went through. You were all tangled inside like the first tree, and that got burned up by the refining fire of your trials. Now, you get new blooms, new life!" It was amazing.

Just days after surgery, the surgeon called our house. We were pretty surprised, as surgeons themselves don't usually call with results, and it also hadn't yet been as long as she'd mentioned we would have to wait to hear back. She began the conversation by reminding me of the nine places on my cervix that she'd originally found cancer. She said, "Jill, I wanted to let you know you did really well." I could tell she was struggling with what she was trying to say. She continued, "When I operated, Jill, every one of those problem areas was already free of cancer. Your cervix was all clear. Your lymph nodes were perfect. Our fears about cancer penetrating the uterine wall and requiring chemo were completely unfounded. In your entire body, we could only find one cancerous spot, and it was barely one millimeter in diameter." That's the thickness of a single guitar string. I was elated! And she was confused—dumbstruck even. God had come through! But she didn't know Him like I did.

The doctor had a question though. "Jill, I can assure you that little string of cancer we found could never have produced the severe symptoms you were experiencing that led us into this whole process. So I have a question for you." I couldn't keep it in anymore, and I burst out, "God did what He said He would! He touched me and healed me!" The physician pressed on. "Yes...but I have to ask you. If God healed you, why did He leave any trace of cancer in your body?" The Holy Spirit had an answer for her though! I had the biggest smile on my face as He told me. I responded gleefully, "Well, God loves you, too. And if you had opened me up and did all this and found nothing, you'd be in pretty big trouble!" She laughed. Then I said, "Did you see the glory?" Her response was hesitant. "I have to admit, I did. I don't understand it, but I saw it." God was using all this. I went on, "When you're ready, go read the book of John. Just start there." What a seed God planted in her life that day! We wonder why we go through things, but we have to learn to trust our Father and His good plans. It's all a journey He's bringing us through.

Chapter 12

God Our Healer

> "When evening had come, they brought to Him many who were demon-possessed. And He cast out the spirits with a word, and healed all who were sick, that it might be fulfilled which was spoken by Isaiah the prophet, saying: 'He Himself took our infirmities and bore our sicknesses.'"—
> Matthew 8:16-17

JESUS REALLY DID COME TO HEAL. When you read the four Gospels in the Bible, you can't leave without the impression that a major portion of Jesus's three years of ministry was spent healing people. The moment Jesus launched into public ministry, He began to get a reputation for restoring physical health. People came to Him with diseases, with pains in various parts of their bodies, with epilepsy, and with paralysis, and He healed all who came. After describing Jesus's baptism in chapter three and his defeat of Satan's temptations in early chapter four, Matthew's narrative immediately picks up with preaching and healing ministry. The Word says, *"And Jesus went about all Galilee, teaching in their synagogues, preaching the gospel of the kingdom, and healing all kinds of sickness and all kinds of disease among the people. Then His fame went throughout all Syria..."* (Matthew 4:23-24a).

Consider what you remember most from your reading of the Gospels. We think of what? The woman with a flow of blood touched the hem of Jesus's garment and was made well. Blind Bartimaeus received his sight as he begged by the roadside outside of Jericho. The paralytic's friends lowered him through a roof where Jesus was teaching, and Jesus both forgave his sins and restored his ability to walk. Then there's Jairus's daughter and Lazarus who were both raised from death—healed even after taking their last breath. And as John says, *"There are also many other things that Jesus did, which if they were written one by one,*

I suppose that even the world itself could not contain the books that would be written" (John 21:25). These memorable moments of healing are just the slightest taste of all that Jesus did to restore the bodies of broken and hurting people. So physical healing must be important to God, right? And if that's the case, can we expect healing when we come to God? Does faith guarantee physical health? Let's look to the Word and the character of God, and let's start at the beginning.

In the beginning, God created the heavens and the earth, and on the sixth day, He made mankind as male and female in His image. When He did that, there was no death in the world. God's life was everlasting, and He had breathed His spirit, His lifeforce, into the man and woman so that they were animated by it. What's more, He had provided a tree of life in the midst of the garden of Eden that would allow the man and woman to live together, with Him, forever. The whole story of the world filled with trouble and pain and death began without any of those things. And knowing that, we can understand something of God's heart for mankind—for us. The worst things we experience were not His intention. He did not birth us for grief, struggle, and pain.

In fact, we even have a promise in the Word that

guarantees us God's intentions haven't changed, no matter what we see around us in the world today. In Revelation 21, at the very end of the Scriptures, God shows us what happens when all the sinning and fighting is done and Jesus has returned. It says:

> *I heard a loud voice from heaven saying, "Behold, the tabernacle of God is with men, and He will dwell with them, and they shall be His people. God Himself will be with them and be their God. And God will wipe away every tear from their eyes; there shall be no more death, nor sorrow, nor crying. There shall be no more pain, for the former things have passed away." Then He who sat on the throne said, "Behold, I make all things new..."* (Revelation 21:3-5).

Did you hear that? There will be *no more* pain. One day, your back won't hurt anymore. One day, it won't be so hard to get around. One day, your heart won't give you trouble. One day, you won't fight to take a breath between coughing fits. One day, the "c" word won't exist. God said so! And you can take that to the bank, because God never lies, and His Word always accomplishes what He sends it out to do (Isaiah 55:11).

What really captures the scene are those last words

from God's own lips, "Behold, I make all things new." The story that started with a new world is going to end with a new world. God isn't going to let the ocean of human failings across history stand in the way of what He set out to do. He's going to accomplish it. So He plans to make all things new. Your frail, broken, aging body will be made new if you trust in Jesus to join Him there on that day. The cracked and crumbling ruins of society will be made new. Fractured relationships between brethren in Christ will be made new. All creation will be restored. God will set all things right! And how is this accomplished? Through Jesus! The mystery of God's will since before time began has been to unite all things in Christ, things in heaven and on earth (Ephesians 1:10). Because Jesus died, condemning sin in the flesh and destroying death itself, and because He rose from the dead to bring life to all that was once dead, all people and things can be restored.

And THAT is what Jesus was sent to do. He began His ministry fulfilling the words of Isaiah, *"The Spirit of the Lord God is upon Me, because the Lord has anointed Me to preach good tidings to the poor; He has sent Me to heal the brokenhearted, to proclaim liberty to the captives, and the opening of the prison to those who are bound"* (Isaiah 61:1, ESV). Jesus came to restore hope to those who had lost it, to restore hearts and bodies to health, and to restore freedom to those who had given it away or had it snatched from them by others or by sin. This passage means a whole lot more than people getting free from demons and physical sickness. After all, everyone Jesus healed eventually died—many doubtless from physical health troubles—and Jesus said that those who had demons driven out could easily end up with more and worse demons in the end (Luke 11:24-26). Jesus did *more* than these things. He set souls free from captivity to sin and set lives loose forever from the pangs of death, and He opened the doors of people's personal spiritual prisons to give them the freedom of the children of God, adopted into the Father's family to reign with Him forever. These works are truly great and lasting. But Jesus *also* meant physical healing was part of what He came to do, as the Word testifies and as His time on earth demonstrates.

What these many truths are saying is this: God cares about *complete* restoration. Wholeness of being is His aim for humanity. He wants us with Him and well. And this isn't just something Jesus showed us for a specific time period that wasn't there before in the heart of God. No, the main purpose in Jesus coming was to reveal the Father to us, so that all might understand who He was, is, and will be. He does not change! (Malachi 3:6, James 1:17) God's Word says, *"God, who at various times and in various ways spoke in time past to the fathers by the prophets, has in these last days spoken to us by His Son, whom He has appointed heir of all things...being the brightness of His glory and the express image of His person"* (Hebrews 1:1-3a). Jesus is the "express image of God's person," helping us understand God's heart. If we meet Jesus, we meet God the Father. This is why when Philip asked to see the Father, Jesus said, *"Have I been with you so long, and yet you have not known Me, Philip? He who has seen Me has seen the Father; so how can you say, 'Show us the Father'?"* (John 14:9). Jesus came to show us God's true nature, and He did it in large part by healing everyone He could find.

This means you and I can look to God's heart as revealed through Jesus to find comfort. We can trust that He intends to heal us. He intends to restore to us all that is lost to us because of this world of sin. And He *will* do it. But sometimes, all is not well until glory. Sometimes, we keep suffering with sickness and pain, and sometimes, people we love die. Sometimes, healing appears to be far away. And we have to understand something. What Jesus did during His earthly ministry as recorded in the Gospels was a *foretaste* of the kingdom that was breaking into the world. As He said to His disciples, the kingdom of God was in the midst of them. He was demonstrating it tangibly before their very eyes, showing them what the future kingdom would be like when there was no more sickness or pain because God's own presence would be there pouring out life and healing forever. And it didn't end when Jesus died and rose! He has become one flesh with His Body, the Church, whom He says is *"the fullness of Him, who fills all in all"* (Ephesians 1:23). That means Jesus is still here on earth today—in you and in me if we trust Him. And He is still committed to the same work. But it is yet a foretaste of a kingdom that is *not yet* fully here. Listen, if the kingdom had come in fullness, every knee would bow and every tongue would confess that Jesus is Lord—today—and evil would STOP! It hasn't. We feel that every day. And that's because the King Himself has not yet returned to vanquish evil completely and to make all things new.

So we find ourselves looking at a God who wants our complete bodily restoration, who still heals today in and through His people, and who promises to fully and finally heal us when the new creation comes—but we suffer some now. Sometimes, our physical suffering is the direct work of Satan's attacks, as Jesus showed us when he healed a crippled woman that He'd said was bound by Satan for 18 years (Luke 13:10-16). And all sickness, death, and pain is an indirect result of Satan's temptation of Adam and Eve, whereby Adam brought sin into the world and death through sin (Romans 5:12). However, it's not as simple as saying we need to cast out demons from every sick person so they'll be well.

Throughout the Word, God demonstrates how He uses physical affliction to discipline His people and judge the nations. The very moment God introduced Himself as Jehovah Rophe, God Our Healer, to the people of Israel, He described in the same breath how He brought disease upon the Egyptians, and He warned His people to listen so they wouldn't face the same fate (Exodus 15:26). Then, once Jesus came and accomplished the work that offered healing to the world, Paul said many of the Corinthian church members were sick and some had died because they weren't honoring Christ when they took communion (1 Corinthians 11:23-34). When you pair that with Paul's admonition to a sick Timothy to take some wine for his frequent ailments (1 Timothy 5:23), we don't get the impression that the early Church believed they could live without health struggles. And this is *not* a cheapening of what Jesus accomplished.

We have to face the whole Word in order to walk rightly by faith in the God of the Word. The reality is, God loves you to death, longs to see you healed and restored in every way, is fully capable of making you physically whole, and yet sometimes waits to heal you until the kingdom fully comes. That's the truth. And it need not lessen our faith or harm our relationship with our heavenly Father. What we have to understand is that the healing ministry Jesus first brought to the world was the beginning of something that would continue to grow until the whole world could be healed when He returns. Not everyone got healed in His day, and not everyone gets healed in our day. But many, many do. And God's heart remains the same. This should give us great comfort as we walk with Him through the trials we face.

The most important thing in all of this is the reason people get healed in the first place. Why does God heal? Love is a major motivation, yes. But Jesus shares something else with us of which we must take note to be able to really grasp His heart. The book of John describes a moment where Jesus heals a man born blind, and it's incredibly enlightening.

> *Now as Jesus passed by, He saw a man who was blind from birth. And His disciples asked Him, saying, "Rabbi, who sinned, this man or his parents, that he was born blind?" Jesus answered, "Neither this man nor his parents sinned, but that the works of God should be revealed in him."* (John 9:1-3)

Then Jesus healed the man, who then told many others about this Jesus who had restored his sight. God demonstrated His time-tested character by bringing hope to a troubled soul through bodily healing, and that gave Him glory! The glory was multiplied exponentially by the man sharing God's works with others afterwards. And somehow, all of that was worth the man *not* being healed his entire life *until* that point. Now, the fellow could have looked back on that moment and wondered why God had allowed him to be blind in the first place, but all that mattered was he was whole and had met a Savior who could restore all things.

It's critical we get this. Life is not about us. Healing is not about us. Our stories are just part of God's great story, and that is not *just* a small thing! We get to be part of reflecting the glorious light of our King who has always been, always will be, and who made the world for Himself and by His power. We will be with Him forever because of the great things He has done, and our time on earth until then is about honoring Him for what He has done and will do for us. Any sickness or pain or other trial we must endure to give Him the glory due His name is worth it, because He is worth it. So we can ask for healing, and we can receive it! But we can also endure suffering for the sake of Him who suffered for us, trusting God's heart for us until we are fully restored, whether that's tomorrow when we wake up or in glory when Jesus returns.

I'm one of those who found healing on this side of glory. Our heavenly Father was gracious enough to display His glory in me by healing me of cancer. And I am SO thankful! Still, even then, I had to go through surgery and quite a process of pain and difficulty. And at the end of the day I was healed partially—almost completely, yes, but partially. And THAT was for God's glory. I got to share God's love with my surgeon because God chose to heal all but 1mm of cancer. And I made it to that moment because He chose to wait and heal me after I had suffered for months. But you know what? I got to share in Christ's sufferings for the sake of His Body, like the Apostle Paul talked about. And now, I get to tell my story to the whole world. I get to tell GOD'S story to the whole world, and His glory is only going to increase. How many people might find hope in His name because of what He did in my life?

So my challenge to you today is this: turn your trials over to God—physical and otherwise. Offer yourself up as a suffering servant to Jesus for the sake of His glory, and ask Him how He can honor His name through what you are facing. And ASK for healing too because you know His heart for you is full restoration. Believe in who He says He is and what He promises to do, while submitting yourself to whatever you must until He returns. And what comes of it will amaze you—and the world.

Prayer Response

"Father, I've suffered a lot in my life. You know. At the same time, I know it pales in comparison to what your Son suffered for me. Please grant me the grace to desire fellowship with you in my sufferings; glorify your Name somehow through what I am facing. Still, Father, I am too weak to keep going like this. I need healing, and I believe you want to restore me completely through your Son's finished work! Jehovah Rophe, God My Healer, I trust your heart for me. Restore me. And give me the strength of soul to bear up until my healing comes. Don't let me dishonor your Name because of my weakness. Let your strength be made perfect in it instead. Help me always to trust your heart enough that I never doubt your love for me when I struggle with health problems. And like the apostle John blessed the church, let me be in good health and let all be well with me. Only you can give us life and hope, both now and in fullness when you return—forever! I pray in Jesus's holy Name. Amen!"

A Word from Jill Falco

First, I want to thank you for reading my story. I knew that the Lord wanted me to be an open book during the sharing of my testimony. Jim told me that if God said it, I should share it!

One of the most important things I wanted to convey was that we have a supernatural God who told us we would see *greater* miracles in our lifetime than when He walked the earth. That is amazing! He *always* answers prayer, even if His answer is not the one we think we should get.

I am grateful God has allowed me to see in the Spirit and understand good and evil in that way, but the greatest miracle of all is the miracle of SALVATION through FAITH! The most amazing thing God does is rescue us and offer us a life of deep, loving union with Him. When we turn to God away from a life lived our own way to accept His way, provided through Jesus's perfect life, sacrificial death, and resurrection, He offers us life everlasting.

When we accept the gift of salvation with the understanding that Jesus died for our sins while suffering on the cross, Jesus unites us with Himself and promises to be with us forever. Choosing to experience eternal life with Jesus by His finished work on our behalf is the greatest decision anyone will ever make.

He is the only true living God! I am thankful that I have seen Jesus in the Spirit and had Him hold me in His arms when I was weak. He is real, loving, kind, and never leaves us or forsakes us. If you have never read a Bible, I challenge you to read the book of John. There is no better love story! And if you feel moved to give your life to Jesus, I urge you to sincerely pray the prayer below.

For Him,

Jill Falco

— Below, you'll find a prayer to help lead you to new life in Christ, if you haven't yet been saved from your life of sin.

This is an example prayer from a heart touched by God's Word. You may pray these words just as they are or let them inspire your heart to speak your own words to God.

Honesty is everything here. This is a commitment, but it's the best decision you'll ever make, and you will be united with God for now and for eternity.—

A Salvation Prayer: "God, I'm a sinner. I've lived my way all my life, and I don't want to anymore. I want your way. I want your Son, Jesus. Thank you for sending Jesus to pay for my sins by His death on the cross. I believe He did that for me. Please cover my sins, forgive me, and save me. I believe Jesus' perfect life will stand in place of my imperfection. And I believe His resurrection will defeat death for me and give me eternal life with You forever. I have decided to follow Jesus—no turning back. In Jesus' Name I pray, amen!"

Connect with Jill

I'm so thankful you've joined me on this journey with the Spirit! You can connect with me via the contact form on my website www.jillfalco.com. On my site, you'll also find an online store for gifts and prophetic art inspired by Holy Spirit.

Please take a look around and enjoy! I paint at conferences, events, church services, and my art studio with worship music. It is an honor to paint what heaven is saying. People have shared with me that the prints carry the same anointing in which it was painted under. It's so exciting!

A Word from Jonathan Macnab

Hello! I hope you've just met with God today. I don't think either Jill or I could have a greater desire for this book than for it to serve as a meeting place between our heavenly Father and His children. It was a tremendous privilege to be part of producing this book with Jill, and all the hours of writing, editing, and spiritual warfare were entirely worth it.

It's a miracle that she and I even met, as my journey with Jesus through North Carolina only stopped at her church doorstep for a few weeks, but she was right there hearing from the Spirit and ready for a sovereign meeting. It didn't take us long to know exactly why we met, and the project was underway. Her story is one that deserves to be told, because God so greatly glorifies His Name in it. And it stands as a living example of the childlike faith for which we all must strive so we can experience the deepest fellowship with our Father in heaven.

If you take nothing else from your reading of this story, pay attention to the Jesus Jill knows, the One who carried her in the sky and went out of His way to show her His love, the One who gave His life on the cross for you and rose from death to give you a chance at lasting hope.

Follow Him, and find life abundant!

For Him,

Jonathan Macnab

Connect with Jonathan

I hope you enjoyed the book! Please support the work by leaving a review at your favorite book retailer.

If you have any thoughts or questions regarding my books, writing project collaboration, or speaking engagements, feel free to reach out via the contact form on my site www.storyreborn.com.

There, you'll also be able to peruse my blog and join my email list to get updates on new books and gain access to book samples or advanced book copies. I look forward to hearing from you!

Help Spread the Word

If you believe in the message of this book or the Scriptures contained within, you can help be a part of increasing the Word of God in the world and increasing the faith that comes through hearing the Word. Please review the book at your favorite book retailer so that the book becomes higher recommended and easier to find for potential readers.

Please also consider some of the following uses:

* Share the online bookstore link (books2read.com/SpiritJourney) on your social media with a personal message about its content.
* Present a print copy to someone you meet out and about or to someone visiting your home.
* Leave a copy in barber shops, waiting rooms, etc.
* Put a print copy in your church library or offer it as a free discipleship resource.
* Forward it to hospitals, to prisons, to sailors, soldiers, firemen, and others with standby time and a need for good material.
* Make a list of friends or acquaintances who should read the book, then send the book to the first named and ask them to pass it on to the second, and so on.

* Call the attention of your local bookseller to it and urge them to carry a line of books from this publisher.
* Read it aloud to your children or other young people.

www.ingramcontent.com/pod-product-compliance
Lightning Source LLC
LaVergne TN
LVHW090115080426
835507LV00040B/892